# The Chanticleer 1994

Christina H. Anderson

Alpha Editions

This edition published in 2020

ISBN : 9789354043680

Design and Setting By
**Alpha Editions**
www.alphaedis.com
email - alphaedis@gmail.com

As per information held with us this book is in Public Domain. This book is a reproduction of an important historical work. Alpha Editions uses the best technology to reproduce historical work in the same manner it was first published to preserve its original nature. Any marks or number seen are left intentionally to preserve its true form.

# THE CHANTICLEER

## 1994

Edited by Christina H. Anderson

Duke University, Durham, North Carolina
To Nannerl O. Keohane, President of the University

# TABLE OF CONTENTS

THE CHANTIC

PROLOGUE

PAGE 6

EVENTS

PAGE 32

ACADEMICS

PAGE 66

ATHLETICS

PAGE 94

PORTRAITS

PAGE 152

RESIDENTIAL LIFE

PAGE 178

GREEK LIFE

PAGE 198

CLASS OF 1994

PAGE 212

EPILOGUE

PAGE 258

# PROLO

GUE

My first year at Duke has been characterized most of all by learning — learning not only new facts, new roads and buildings, a new set of names and faces, but also a new set of traditions, signals, moods and expectations.

Institutions are made up of such things, as all of you have learned in your own time at Duke. Like you, I came to Duke with some basic expectations formed by the image of the University in the world outside. I discovered, as I am sure you have, that some of these expectations were well-grounded, and others were way off base.

I had thought of Duke as a southern university — and discovered that while this is true in some basic geographical sense, Duke is far more national, cosmopolitan, even international that I had expected. I had thought of Duke mainly in undergraduate terms — and discovered that the undergraduate historic core is much more richly balanced by the graduate and professional schools than a cursory familiarity might indicate. I had thought of Duke as a place where basketball reigns supreme for several months a year — and discovered that people outside can only imagine what it is really like to be part of this university during basketball season, what a totally and fiercly dedicated institution we become.

My memories of my first year at Duke are richly varied and overwhelmingly positive, as I hope your memories of your Duke years will be as well.

I remember vividly my first day in office, July 1, 1993 — how hot it seemed outside, how thick the trees were around the windows at my house and in my office, how sultry it felt, compared with the softer New England summer to which I had become accustomed. I recall confronting mountains of papers, reports, memoranda, lists of people and committees, accounts of work that someone had been waiting impatiently for months for me to do, and wondering if I would ever be able to chart my way through it all successfully and learn enough about Duke to make a difference as its president before it was time to retire. I recall how many buses there were outside my window, and how everyone at Duke seemed to be moving back and forth by means of this ecologically ambiguous form of transportation.

I recall the end of that first day, when for the first time I heard the carillon at five o'clock from the Chapel Tower. Since I love carillon music, I opened my windows (defying both the sultry weather and the buses) to hear it better, but still only with half my consciousness. Suddenly I was wrested back into full attention by a familiar and totally unexpected tune. "I must be hallucinating," I said to myself. "That sounds like the Wellesley alma mater [which is hardly a familiar favorite tune]." And then there was another piece, which I surmised must be Duke's alma mater, and I realized that our splendid carilloneur Sam Hammond had made the most graceful possible transition for me from loyalty to my old institution to loyalty to the new.

There were many other high points in the weeks and months that followed. My first visit to the Marine Lab in Beaufort, including a trip out on the research vessel *Cape Hatteras,* and the dolphins that escorted us back into the harbor. My first visit to the Medical Center, watching open heart surgery and meeting the nurses and docs and technicians and support people on the wards. The opening week of school, convocation in the Chapel, greeting all the eager new students and their families. The inauguration — how magnificent the day was, from weather to the enthusiastic participation and palpable affectionate support from so many people at Duke and members of the University community.

My first time as President in Cameron Indoor Stadium, then all the other times that followed, Charlotte, and Knoxville, and Charlotte again, sharing both triumphs and defeats with an extraordinary group of athletes and Coach K. My first tree-lighting, and first Christmas Eve Service in Duke Chapel, mysterious and brilliant in the candlelight. My first spring in Durham, watching the progressive loveliness of the flowers, trees, and grasses. My first Commencement weekend, sharing in those high-spirited festivities with so many eager newly-minted graduates and their families.

I recall also more familiar routines and habits. Running or cycling in Duke Forest as a refreshment of the spirit as well as the body — seeing a blue heron, a hawk; hearing the spring creepers, the awakening birds, a morning dove, an eerie but neighborly owl who took up residence close outside my bedroom window. Greeting my co-workers every morning, people from public safety, grounds and housekeeping, secretaries and deans and vice-presidents. Picking up the morning papers, knowing that it was almost certain that there would be something about Duke, hoping it would be mostly good news instead of bad, hoping that the *Chronicle* would have written the story I wanted to see rather than the one that made me anxious, and generally batting about .500.

I recall good conversations with so many of you, students, faculty, trustees, and staff — over lunches in the Oak Room or the Faculty Commons Room, ice cream in the dorms, elegant dinner parties, at sports events, by electronic mail, before or after meetings, sitting in my office, or just passing in the Quad.

Of course there are some things about Duke that I hope we can change. I have talked with many of you this year about what some of those might be. I sometimes get impatient, as I know many of you do, that change appears to come so slowly, and to take so long. But there are also many things that it is important to protect about Duke, many unique distinctions about this place.

One of the things I have heard expressed by students and alumni most often, and most consistently, this year, is a burning desire to "let Duke be Duke," to conserve the special character of this place. This is a good goal to have: and to fulfill it, we need to be even clearer than we have been in the past about what precisely it is that makes Duke Duke, and which parts of our special character are most important to protect. To ensure that Duke continues to live up to its traditions and its dreams does not mean trying to hold it frozen in some dimly imagined past. It means deciding which aspects of our university are most essential to its character, and how we can protect and enhance them in the years ahead. Our purpose should be to think boldly not just about what Duke is like today, but about what is fundamentally best about Duke far in the future.

I am glad to have shared this year with all of you. I know that this volume will be for you, as it is for me, the permanent record of an exceptional moment in our lives.

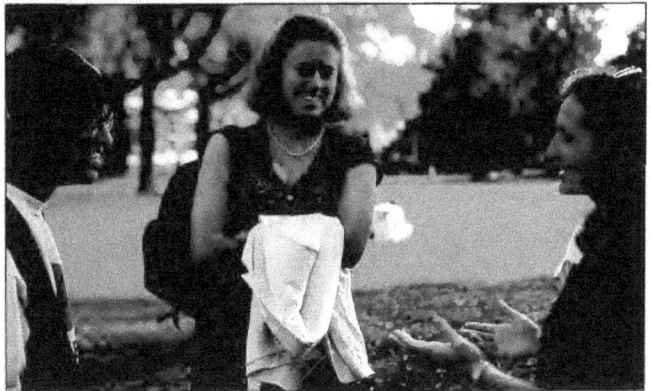

Prologue

# EVEN

TS

# Inauguration of Nannerl O. Keohane

# Renovation of Lilly Library

# Take Back the Night

# Naomi Wolf

"We must dare to assume full responsibility as well as ask for full rights, because human status brings with it the ineradicable moral weight of making choices—including the most wicked ones. And feminism should not mean being a saint. It should mean owning one's own demonic, angelic soul."     -from her book, Fire With Fire

# Step Show

# American Indian Dance Theater

# Shelby Steele

On Thursday, November 4, 1993, Dr. Shelby Steele came to Duke University to speak about racism. Best known for the piece he did for a Sixty Minutes episode on race relations at Duke, Dr. Steele directed his speech toward problems concerning African American relations. An English professor at San Jose University, he said that education is the key to wiping out racism.

# Ken Kesey

On Tuesday, November 16, 1993, author Ken Kesey read a selection from his most recent literary accomplishment, Sailor Song, to Duke University. Mr. Kesey is most noted for his literary classic, One Flew Over the Cuckoo's Nest. Through his storytelling, he conveyed what it means to be a warrior, which he defined as someone who stands up for what they believe in.

# Janet Reno

On Saturday, January 22, 1994, on behalf of the Major Speakers and the Law School's Frontiers of Legal Thought Conference, Attorney General Janet Reno urged the future leaders of America to take a holistic and firm stand against crime. According to her, key issues the American legal system must face are rehabilitation and prevention. She stressed the importance of family values and provided anecdotes from her own childhood.

# Paul Tsongas

On Thursday, February 24, 1994, Paul Tsongas, ex-Massachusetts senator, ex-Presidential candidate, and current co-chairman of the Concord Coalition, came to Duke University. He spoke about his plan to reduce the national deficit. The plan includes a flat national income tax to alleviate the expanding debt.

# Mardi Gras

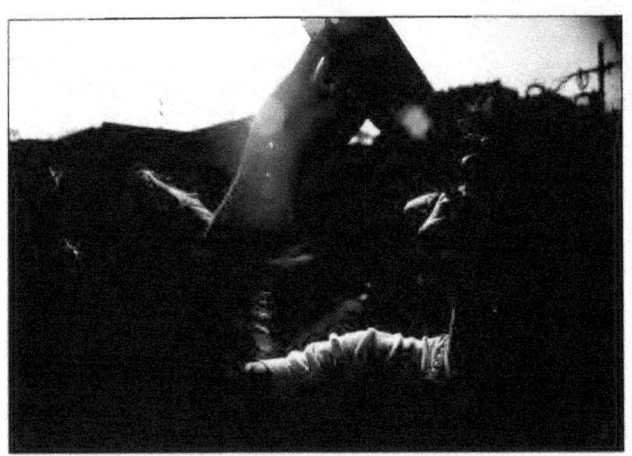

# Springfest

# Pitchforks

# The Dave Matthews Band

# Widespread Panic

# The Samples

# Lemonheads

# Arrested Development

# Mike Krzyzewski

On Thursday, November 11, 1993, Men's Basketball coach Mike Krzyzewski gave a "basketball preview" to discuss the upcoming season with Duke students. His speech about the team and its goals was followed by a question and answer period. The questions were directed towards his expectations for the four new freshmen. Students wanted to know how much the freshmen could contribute, and how they would be used in the Duke Blue Devil's game plan.

# Oliver Stone

On Friday, December 3, 1993, the film maker Oliver Stone spoke about his past films including his latest, <u>Heaven and Earth</u>, the third film in his Vietnam trilogy. He also addressed the present state of American society; he thinks that Americans are too busy with technology to get in touch with their spiritual side. He tries to make movies that capture the spiritual side of humanity. Finally, he urged the audience to be truthful even if it means challenging political and historical standards.

# Joe Clark

In February, the motivational speaker Joe Clark spoke about race relations and education in the United States. Joe Clark was the principal portrayed by Morgan Freeman in the movie Lean on Me. Through stories that illustrated his ideas, he stressed that African Americans should stop killing each other and instead work constructively together to elevate themselves. He also condemned affirmative action, saying that it lowers society's expectations of African Americans. Additionally, Mr. Clark said that there should be universal choices for children's education so that children who live in the city can have the same educational opportunities as children in the suburbs.

# Cornel West

On Thursday April 7th, 1994, Harvard University professor Cornel West came to Duke University. At a two day conference on Jews and Christians in the South, he spoke to students about Black-Jewish relations. He encouraged and challenged the two groups to work together to overcome their hardships.

# Final Four

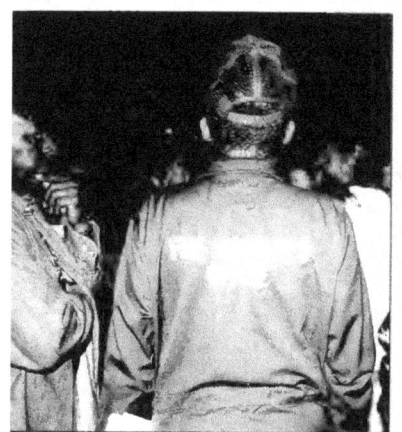

Events•49

# Danny Glover

# Felix Justice

# Benjamin Chavis, Jr.

# Benjamin Barber

# Adam Sandler

# Tom DeLuca

# Hoof 'n' Horn

# Duke Drama

No Exit

# Kaspar

# Noises Off

McTeague

# Myrtle Beach

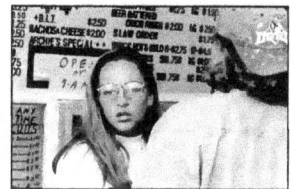

# Graduation

## Judy Woodruff

# May 8, 1994

# 1993-1994

*If anything, the lower turnout is probably due to the good weather we are having. That probably deterred people from getting out to vote.*
Trinity junior John Tolsma, DSG president-elect, on yesterday's low voter turnout

*It is unfair for one commodity to be singled out and leave something like alcoholic beverages unscathed.*
Rep. Tim Valentine, D-N.C., on a proposed $1.25 per pack cigarette tax

*We've been calling [Grant Hill] the 'Dog Catcher' the past couple of days.*
Junior center Cherokee Parks on senior co-captain Grant Hill, who will go head-to-head with Glenn 'Big Dog' Robinson when the men's basketball team takes on Purdue Saturday for the right to go to the Final Four

*Sometimes you play well, and you lose.*
Men's head basketball coach Mike Krzyzewski

*No team that I've coached has had more heart than this basketball team.*
Mike Krzyzewski, men's head basketball coach, on the 1993-1994 team at the rally in Cameron Tuesday

*It's probably worse than it looks.*
Linda Carl, director of student health, on survey results showing 47 percent of University students binge drink

*I'm Catholic, and I just don't feel like watching that sort of thing.*
Trinity freshman Holly Guss on a plan to bring a male dancer to Jarvis

*Life without kegs is like life without chicks.*
Trinity junior Ken Brunt, on IFC's new alcohol policy banning kegs

*Bill Lane has been a loyal, generous alumnus of the University and [member of the] trustees.*
Board of Trustees chair John Chandler on a trustee convicted of bank fraud

*Let me tell you something. We've won 13 games in a row. We plan to make it a 14th. We won our last game. Duke lost theirs. We're going to Florida to win. We're not worried about just having a good time.*
Robert Moreland, Texas Southern men's basketball head coach

*I think it is excellent.*
Engineering sophomore Gavin Kistner on the computerized ACES listings

*This serves to underscore the problem that's out there-discrimination.*
Graduate student Michael Pino on the covering of the slurs painted on the East Campus bridge

*I think the way to deal with the problem is not to whitewash the problem... Should we have black people paint their skin white so you don't have racial tensions?*
Trinity junior Nate Harshman on the possibility of revoking freshman car privileges

*We will enforce the law in such a manner to maintain control and minimize injury.*
Chief Lewis Wardell of Duke Public Safety on Saturday's celebration

*I've gotten bored with the same rhetor Find something else to do. Find some other way to articulate your homophobia, if it's something you wa to cling to.*
Trinity senior Todd Presner, DGL chair, on people who use the Bible condemn homosexuality

*We feel like we're being talked to and listened to, but nothing's being done.*
Maurice Corders, member of the Medical Center minority employee task force

*In 1992, the American people deman that we change. We replaced drift an deadlock with renewal and reform.*
President Clinton

*Just turn it over to the prosecutor an let him find out.*
Democratic Sen. Daniel Patrick Moynihan of New York, calling f President Clinton to allow an out side prosecutor to investigate his involvement in an Arkansas real estate venture linked to a failed savings and loan

*We hear gun shots pretty regularly.*
Trinity senior Nicole van Nood o her fiance's apartment near East Campus

*There is a possibility that someone c go to Duke and...never go on a date.*
Wendy Luttrell, assistant profess of the practice in the sociology department

*Every place you step or walk there i hole.*
Engineering junior Dan Carrizos construction near North Campu

# On The Record

bottom line is in the win-loss
...mn and I have not been able to get
...job done. I take full responsibility
...that.
...tball coach Barry Wilson, on the
...son for his resignation

...e legal system needs to hear] all
...es—rich, poor; young, old; hetero-
...ual, homosexual; black, white. If you
...injustice, speak up. If you see
...rimination, speak up. If you see
...ence, speak up.
...es Smith, third-year law student

...t's splendid news.
...sident Nan Keohane on the
...ction of a University student for
...hodes Scholarship

...ink that changing our letters, philan-
...py or colors won't change the
...men, and our ideals from the start
...stay with us regardless of the letters
...our sweatshirts.
...nity senior Ginger Fay, a member
Theta Beta Sigma sorority

...n't see any rationale for [major]
...nges...I think we got it right.
...ademic Council chair Richard
...ton, on the proposed harassment
...icy

...ounds like it doesn't give the victim
...arassment much power.
...nity junior Deborah Forbes, on
...proposed harassment policy

...s make the campus more cohesive.
...s bond the campus together.
...nity sophomore Alli McCoy

...ny opinion, in certain respects,
...stern civilization is better than other
...lizations throughout the world.
...tor Strandberg, English professor

I got a taste of Duke that showed me the true mentality of the professors, [especially] the older professors, and it saddened me.
Anji Malhotra, Trinity sophomore

I don't see how they can even pretend to represent student views to the trustees.
Engineering senior David Lott on DSG officials supporting East as all-freshmen

Being a good Christian, I allowed North Carolina to win a national championship. This year's different—I haven't even been to church yet.
Coach Mike Krzyzewski, on the men's basketball team

I think it's a sad day for Duke. It's appalling.
Ole Holsti, professor of political science and supporter of Timothy Lomperis, assistant professor of political science, who lost his tenure appeal to the Board of Trustees

These will be hard times, but there will also be many joyous times.
President Nan Keohane in her first Convocation address

I have done everything in my power to keep people out of there.
Margaret Coile, owner of the quarry where Brian Wright may have drowned

She didn't want to stick her head out. She walked a fine line; she didn't say anything too drastic.
Ben Feldman, Trinity '90, on President Nan Keohane's speech to alumni Thursday night

She said more in 45 minutes than most people say in a lifetime.
Horace Fowler, Trinity '30, on the same address

[This inauguration] is a great occasion, an occasion that the University ought to have to come together and redefine the direction of the University.
President Emeritus Terry Sanford

All around the country, I see people turning away from change.
President Clinton in a speech at UNC's bicentennial celebration yesterday

The goal the faculty set five years ago was laudable, but unrealistic as a policy.
Provost Thomas Langford, on the Academic Council's five-year resolution to hire at least one black faculty member in each department by 1993

The Clocktower Quad has miraculously turned into Tiananmen Square.
Trinity sophomore Kevin McGinnis on Public Safety's fire prevention efforts

I can go back to doing what I was doing, and that is indeed a relief.
Eric Lincoln, retired University professor, on being found innocent of attempted rape and guilty of misdemeanor assault and battery

The time has come to kick off all fraternities...We should at least expect [living groups] to have the same standards as a sleazy, all-night bar.
Margaret McKean, associate professor of political science, on the campus' intellectual climate

cited from The Chronicle, vol. 89, 1993-94

# ACADE

MICS

### Marion Shepard
Professor, Mechanical Engineering & Materials Science
Associate Dean, School of Engineering

Ava LaVaonne Vinesett
Instructor, African Dance Technique
Dance Department

### Hans J. Van Miegroet
Assistant Professor in the History of Art
Director, Duke Foreign Academic Program in the Netherlands

Susan Willis
Associate Professor, Department of English

E. Roy Weintraub
Acting Dean of the Faculty of Arts and Sciences
Professor, Department of Economics

P. Aarne Vesilind & The Lorax
Professor, Environmental Engineering

Richard A. White
Dean of Trinity College & Vice Provost for Undergraduate Education
University Distinguished Service Professor, Department of Botany

### George C. Wright
Professor, African & Afro-AmericanStudies Program

Bruce Payne
Lecturer, Public Policy Studies

### Martina Bryant
Associate Dean, Trinity College of Arts and Sciences
Adjunct Associate Professor
Program IN Education

### Marcia Lind
**Assistant** Professor, Department of Philosophy

### Stephen A. Wainwright
James B. Duke Professor, Department of Zoology
Executive Director, Bio-Design Studio

**Frances Valdes**
Campus Coordinator for Student Action with Farmworkers

### Norman Keul
Assistant Dean, Trinity College of Arts and Sciences
Director, Pre-Major Advising Center

John Lebar
Associate Professor, Health, Physical Education and Recreation

## Merril Shatzman
Associate Professor of the Practice, Department of Art
Assistant Professor of the Practice of Printmaking

## William Noland
Associate Professor of the Practice, Department of Art

# Phi Beta Kappa

Amy Marie Allshouse, Edward Arnold Amley, Jr., Eric William Amundson, Erik Stephen Benson, Michael J. Bingle, Susan Ilene Brown, René Elizabeth Browne, Daniel Joseph Calhoun, William Harrison Carter, Jill Heath Cartwright, Marc Andrew Cavan, Christina May-ying Chan, Elizabeth Lewis Chandler, Eric Daniel Chason, T Ann Connors, Kristin Scott Crosland, Nina Kavsy Dastur, Jeffrey Charles Domina, Kelly Eamon Dowd, James Edward Duncan, Thomas Norman Felgner, Bevin Eileen Franks, James Robert Funk, Ronald James Gerstle, Michael W. Goodman, Brooke A. Hanaway, Joseph C. Ho, David Jeffrey Horowitz, Gregory Owen Kaden, Katherine Phyllis Kadison, Irene Kaplan, John L. Kelley, David Guy Kirsch, Adam Nathan Klein, Stacy N. Klei Jeffrey Aaron Komisarof, Tonia Marie Korves, Joseph Louis Lichtenberger, Jr., Michaela Louise Long, Todd M thew Lukasik, Juliana Lynn MaGill, Jennifer S. McCall, Suzanne Chopin Michelson, Michelle Elizabeth Middle Joseph Michael Milano, John Todd Miranowski, Kimberly Dawn Mirsky, Romana Moezzi, Mark James Monta Richard Edward Anthony Morris, Evan McLaurin Mueller, Chris Myers, Nancy Chapman Orr, Susan Sarah Ph Gabriel E. Pulido, Warren Lewis Ratliff, Bryan Thomas Raynor, Jennifer Lee Reilly, Nancy L. Reynolds, Leonar Victor Rutgers, Danielle Alisa Salus, Neil S. Siegel, Brad Mitchell Snyder, Jocelyn Sharyn Sperling, Travis Lane Stork, Alison Mann Stuebe, Kristen MArie Thompson, Courtney Dawn Thornburg, Susan Torres, Julie Beth W Jeffrey Greg Weiss, Michael Earl Wenthe, Mark Douglass Whitaker, Samuel Gates Williamson, Jeffrey Todd Wingfield, David Wong, Pamela Lynn Yount

...vid Preston Ayers, Shannon Michael Barrett, Amy Lynn Blair, Kurt Michael Bloomhuff, Joseph Michael ...llinger, Jr., Jeffrey Ford Brent, Alisha Lauren Brosse, John Cardosa II, David A. Cooper, Mark Judson Cooper, ...dia Ruth Coulter, James Patrick Creighton, Catherine M. Crutcher, Pamela Anne Daquila, Michael Anthony ...auphinais, Jr., Robert Tate Duck, Christopher Stewart Endy, Christopher S. Ennen, John David Germanotta, ...awn Louise Gerth, Joshua Lawrence Goldberg, Mark A. Golden, Michael Richard Gustafson II, Scott E. ...arrington, Christopher L. Holley, Amy Elizabeth Hood, M. Joy Jacobs, Janet Elise Johnson, Laura Ruth Jones, ...ul Kelleher, Chang Ook Kim, Simon SungYul Kim, James Allen Kong, Mark Edward Kraynak, Douglas Gary ...chtman, Richard K. Lin, Robin Lynn Maloof, Kristine K. Mavis, Mark David Miller, Jennifer Robin Mohr, Suk Jin ...oon, Lee Katherine Moore, Sandra P. Moreira, Frances Elizabeth Naisang, Dmitry Nemirovsky, Carolyn Eve ...obel, Corey Shane O'Hern, James M. Peppe, Melanie S. Pogach, Michael Lee Anthony Reams, Bethany Sharon ...icks, Rachel Lynne Sagan, Ryan Thomas Scarborough, Jay Whitney Scheerer, Laura J. Schick, Inara K. Scott, Mark ...iristopher Sims, Jonathan B. Slagel, Carsten Meyer Sorenson, Rebecca Frances Stults, Nancy Elizabeth Torre, Blair ...lizabeth Weigle, Brian Stryker Weinstein, Amy Wenzel, Bridget Claire Wiater, Steven Dale Winch, Rachel Linda ...inokur, Marc I. Zemel, Richard P. Zimering

# Beaufort

## Fall

# Spring

# Study Abroad

France

Australia

Cameroon

Ecuador

Germany

New Zealand

Italy

China

# Our Half of the Deal

Ronald Reagan has recently reminded us that he knew Thomas Jefferson. On the face of it, who can doubt him? Sad to say-while I first visited Duke University in 1943 and returned as an undergraduate from 1951 to 1955-even I can't claim to have known James Buchanan Duke. The loss is mine. Evidence for a full picture of him is provided by our colleague Robert Durden in his volume The Dukes of Durham and in his forthcoming and fascinating The Launching of Duke University.

The two books combine to suggest in Mr. Duke a steeltrap mind of size, ceaseless complexity and magnetism-even occasional charm. And a reading of the indenture by which he established his endowment sixty-eight years ago tomorrow shows in a few passages of bareboned eloquence the uncluttered mind of its source-a man born only a few miles from here, who made good worldwide, planned his mammoth benefaction with deliberate care over many years and who, at the very least, knew what he wanted.

In the indenture, J.B. Duke signed his name to a paragraph of specifications for a new university. However influenced the passage was by lawyers cautious to the point of paralysis or by President Few of Trinity College, here are the specifications as Mr. Duke agreed to phrase them (and note the delicacy with which he "requests" and "advises" his successors-if I were giving millions of dollars to a small college in my birthplace, I suspect I'd employ verbs like "require" and "direct"):

*I have selected Duke University as one of the principal objects of this trust because I recognize that education, when conducted along sane and practical, as opposed to dogmatic and theoretical, lines, is, next to religion, the greatest civilizing influence. I request that this institution secure for its officers, trustees and faculty men of such outstanding character, ability and vision as will insure its attaining and maintaining a place of real leadership in the educational world, and that great care and discrimination be exercised in admitting as students only those whose previous record shows a character, determination and application evincing a wholesome and real ambition for life. And I advise that the courses at this institution be arranged, first, with special reference to the training of preachers, teachers, lawyers and physicians, because these are most in the public eye, and by precept and example can do most to uplift mankind, and second, to instruction in chemistry, economics and history, especially the lives of the great of the earth, because I believe that such subjects will most help to develop our resources, increase our wisdom, and promote human happiness.*

What J.B. Duke *said* he wanted, or hoped for, then is clear in general and is often quoted with little reflection on state occasions hereabouts, though he stipulated that the whole long document be read aloud to the trustees annually a request that I'm told is still honored.

A clever fantasist might amuse us by guessing at what J.B. Duke would make of his creature had he survived the trials of the twentieth century to stand here today. But I'll decline that impersonation and hope that it won't prove entirely unwelcome on a grateful occasion if I, as a witness the past four local decades, glance my balance-sheet of hits and mis especially those misses which I suspect would have given Mr. D painful and very likely impatien pause: in the indenture he after gave his trustees power to suspe payments, at their will, to the U versity.

Short of a suicidal attempt examine myself and my faculty colleagues as "men of...outstand character, ability and vision" (ar yes, I hear the absence of the wo *women* from that time-locked phrase), I join with pleasure in t growing sense throughout Ame and a good part of the world th with certain desert treks occasio by war, short funds or an exces folly-the University faculty has grown in responsible intellectu daring and professional stature point at which we may *begin* at to think of ourselves as a first-r academy, presumably the your

## by Reynolds Price

h in the world.

That anyhow has been the m of our recent campaign for ital endowment; and I've more n once endorsed the claim, while etly muffling (like a kinsman sessed of good family values) my ervations about this or that pro- m, this or that howling banshee olleague.

I even try to believe, admit- ly with a frozen smile, the annual ıouncement by our admissions ce that this September's crop of hmen is more beautiful-in mind, ly and soul-and better equipped neet the faculty's challenge than previous generation. But be- th the grin I'm unavoidably alling my certainty that the five usand Duke students of my lergraduate years-the early 0s-gloried in a proportionally ater number of absolutely first- e student minds and that fruitful sonal exchanges between stu- ıts and teachers were far more ımon in those days.

Anyone in search of face- ing explanations for our gradual ition of that splendid compound ght say that the 1950s were more pitious years for white middle- ss public education in America. ey were also years in which, as Duke clearly intended, the iversity more easily wooed and n the exceptionally intelligent, bitiousand almost never wealthy ite students of its own region-both the upper and the deep South.

Despite recent efforts to repair that neglect, the ongoing absence of so many of those promis- ing Southerners-of every race and every degree of income-is partly owing to a breakdown of regional boundaries throughout the nation and partly to our steeply rising tuition. But most sadly the absence of those young Southerners among us is owing to this Unversity's inexplicable loss of will to find the means of supporting those needy students of North Carolina and the South who have earned the right to come here but cannot. I date that loss of will to the early 1960s.

So for more than three de- cades, that failure has not only sent most of the best Southern high- school graduates elsewhere-espe- cially to Chapel Hill where the Morehead Foundation skims a drastic share of the cream of the state, the South and the nation-it has also deprived us of the benign role so explicitly intended for us in forming the future leaders of our time and place. Our benighted politicians and voters are in part our children-our abandoned children.

I'm aware too that, while I encounter in my classes each year a nexus of extraordinary students who keep me teaching, I likewise encoun- ter-and all my classes are elective- the stunned or blank faces of stu- dents who exhibit a minimum of preparation or willingness for what I think of as the high delight and life- enduring pleasure of serious conver- sation in the classsroom and else- where.

Disturbingly often I'm left wondering why a particularly life- less student-one so apparently vacant of Mr. Duke's "real ambition for life"-is present in a university that affirms its luxury of choice and its stringent standards. Whose rightful place is that dullard usurp- ing? My baffled curiousity is by no means eccentric in me.

If we are getting the students we claim to deserve-our earned share of the most intelligent, original and ambitious American high- school graduates-then why do I hear so many colleagues whom I know to be dedicated teachers share the same puzzlement; and why do so many long-time members of the faculty agree that our standards of grading have steadily inflated in recent years? A teacher who grades the students of the nineties as realisti- cally as he did in the 1950s or sixties will face a roomful of empty desks at the start of next term.

Anyone present here today who has not recently spent sus- tained time in a Duke classroom and who doubts my word owes him- or herself an unobtrusive campus tour. Before I suggest a few stops on your route, let me forestall any question of my devotion to the place by stating the obvious-that I've happily chosen to spend my life here and that I'm certain you'll find rewarding sights. You'll witness many probing, enlightening, even pleasing investigations of the urgent mysteries of *Homo sapiens*-investigations conducted by alert and communicative young men and women. You'll likewise witness, among all ages, exchanges of magnanimous courtesy and mutual profit.

But you'll find other sights that breed concern. Visit especially those classes in which a teacher encourages student discussion and is frequently met by a speechless majority who are either lost in riveting meditations of their own, too precious to expose, or have simply never bothered learning to talk in a challenging forum. You'll also note occasional teachers who waltz alone in self-intoxication before their ready but unfed students.

Then walk your attentive self through the quads. Stand at a bus stop at noon rush-hour; roam the reading rooms of the libraries in the midst of term and the panic of exams. Lastly, eat lunch in a dining hall and note the subjects of conversation and the words employed in student discussion (I'm speaking mostly of undergraduates but not exclusively). Try to conceal your consternation at what is often the main theme of discourse-something much less interesting than sex and God, the topics of *my* time. If for instance you can eat a whole meal in a moderately occupied Duke dining hall without transcribing a certain sentence at least once, I'll treat you to the legal pain reliever of your choice. The sentence runs more or less like this, in male *or* female voice-"I can't believe how drunk I was last night."

Considering that the social weekends of many students now begin-indeed are licensed by us to begin-at midday on Thursday and continue through the morning hours of Monday (as they never did in the old days of "country club" Duke), maybe the sentence is inevitable-at least in the bankrupt America we're conspiring to nurture so lovingly and toward which we blindly, or passively anyhow, wave our students.

But how vehemently I doubt that we ought to accept such a message as normal fare in a place as honored as this by a huge gift for doing better with our botched human genes. And how bitterly that impoverished sentence in the mouths of students flies as the banner of the University's remaining enormous failure to them and to J.B. Duke's intention.

That failure proceeds from us all-from the Board of Trustees and the resident administration down through the permanent faculty and the youngest instructor to the students themselves (they join us after all at official voting age). And the failure can be stated quickly-*All of us, in long collusion, have failed to exert a sustained and serious attempt to nurture the literal heart of a great university.* That heart, in the premier universities of America and the world, consists of two things—

First, an environment that is suited for and continuously encouraging to the more or less constant discussion of serious matters and

Second, an atmosphere that awards itself a steady supply of human beings (students, faculty, other staff) who are fitted to converse with one another on serious matters or are willing to learn how.

Am I asking for something the Duke indenture warns against, world of grinding abstract study and a social life built entirely on books? Do we want a place crowded with that dark dread of admissions offices-the *not* well-rounded student? By no means (though all my most rewarding students have been not-well-rounded). The serious dialogue proceeds through the year at all superb institutions worldwide is each of us knows, not a joyless dialogue. On the contrary, such useful discourse is the direct product of the highest human skill; and its large rewards at the simplest level are as exhilarating as Olympic gymnastics.

Like many of you, I've had the luck to spend long stretches of my life in universities where human discourse was centered on the communication of adult thought about matters of enduring interest. I've also had a simultaneous lot of the best fun of my life in such places-pleasure, love and lasting friendship-and Duke at times has been of those places, as it still can be best today. But our best is still too rare an achievement.

As I debated a theme for today and asked a number of current undergraduates for a personal list of local hits and misses, the invariable refrain came to this- h our many causes for gratitude, the thing that holds us back by the ute at Duke is the prevailing cloud difference, of frequent hostility, to a ghtful life. If the students are hful, and I'm sure that they are, ve partly wasted years of their s; and we owe them recompense- ot at once, then at least to their nger siblings and children.

Grant, for the moment, that e students are more than *half* t, where do we turn to redeem wrong? And what do we do by of repair? The question has eated generations of us; and ugh I've participated here since I eighteen in numerous student- faculty-conceived discussion ups, coffees, wine and cheese ties, dorm courses, picnics, rnight seminars beside Lake hie, I've seen each initiative die lack of commitment or continuity he part of all involved. I'm long e certain that our failure pro- ds from a lack of courage to front the failure.

I wish I could offer a blue- nt today for starting at once on confrontation. It will be a giant- rk for everyone here and for long rs to come. But I may have the t of, if not a vision then maybe a nting; and on the occasion of nder's Day, I'll take a last risk. If ere as wise as William P. Few if an equivalent of James B. e entrusted me with many lion dollars, how would I and my eagues begin to use it? I could e they'd join me in an earth- ving act which this University

has delayed many decades and for lack of which it has punished all its members.

We'd take firm steps to move out briskly every fraternity and sorority among us; they would not return. I was once a member of a fraternity that survives on this campus. I enjoyed the laughter in the days before alcohol became our grim solvent; but the uses of such organizations-play and violence and the occasional charitable project-are automatic functions of an animal species as social as our own. And our present fraternities and sorori- ties, grotesque relics as they are of nineteenth-century small rural colleges, have long since ceased to serve any role not better served by means less expensive, in every sense, of the University's time and life-blood. Worse, they're our main force for division and waste-waste of the crucial youth of our students and what their elders might learn from them.

Freed of that burden, we'd move with deliberate speed to organize life throughout the Univer- sity on a residential college model. We'd redesign or rearrange indi- vidual quads and buildings, each with the shortest corridors possible, with private bedrooms for every student and with a dining room in each quad where students could meet like sane adult members of a group dedicated to legitimate prin- ciples of thoughtful social life, punc- tuated by normal bouts of revel.

We already have the seeds of such change in the arts and lan- guage dorms, the interesting anoma-

lies of Epworth and the Round Table. We'd work to find even more promising means of merging the latent minds and energies of this now-scattered place into enviable groups of women and men-in- formed citizens, friends and lovers in a fruitful place.

Mountains of cash would be spent in the effort. It would take us years, but years are precisely what a university has in plenty, and we've proved our skill in raising Himalayas of money. If we actually want a great university-for our- selves, our students and the world- and if we want it hard enough to make a start now, then in-say-a decade I strongly suspect that an- other member of this family could rise at Founder's Day, or sit like me, and inform the recumbent James B. Duke that his unimaginable gener- osity had finally built a place more useful than he imagined: a diverse community, shedding at least a civilized light.

May some new benefactor hear of the need and endow us now for a next huge step-our half of the deal J.B. Duke made. Failing that, we can start with what we've got, here at the end of this tired millenium, and take the first steps toward opening the long-buried vein of human ore we've yet to deserve. Our first need, after all, is mere courage; the second is vision, another free gift. We could reach and take both.

-from Reynolds Price's Founder's Day address at the Founder's Day Convocation, December 1993.

TICS

# Football

# Women's Soccer

# Men's Soccer

# Field Hockey

Athletics•105

# Swimming

# Wrestling

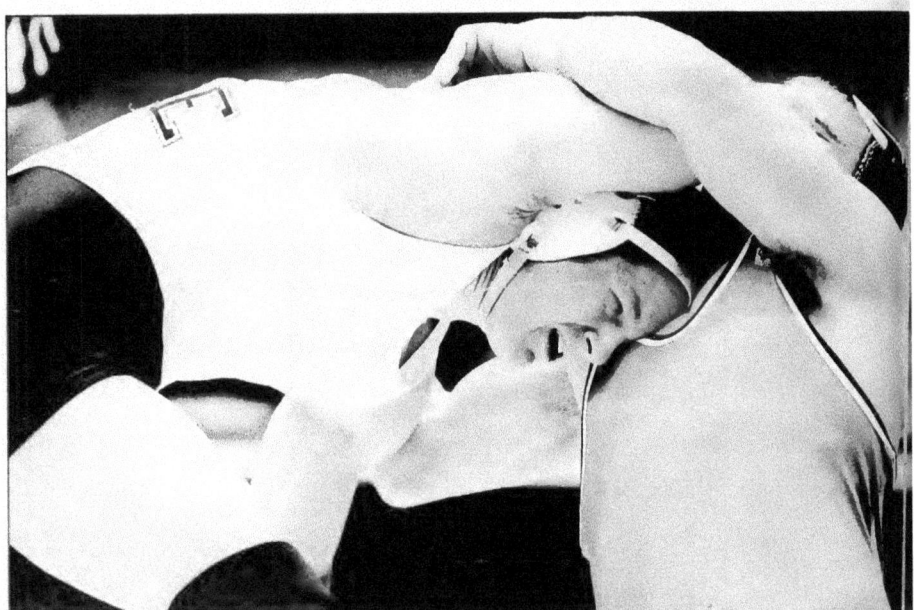

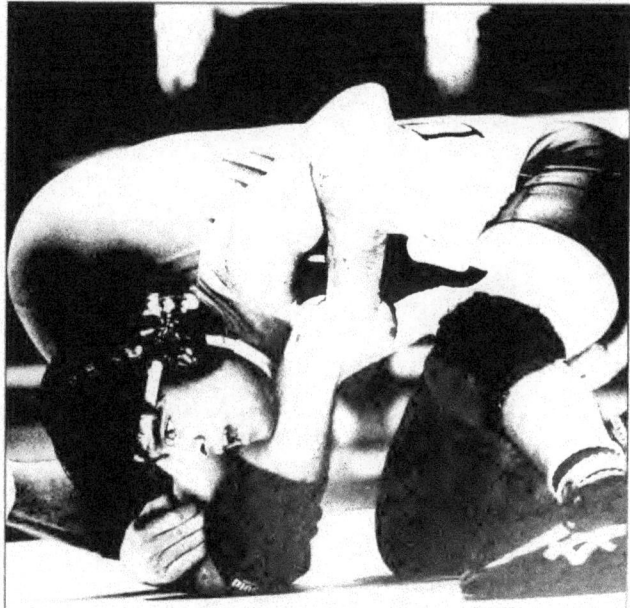

Athletics•109

# Volleyball

# Women's Basketball

# Men's Basketball

Athletics•125

# Track & Field

Athletics•129

# Women's Tennis

# Men's Tennis

# Women's Golf

# Men's Golf

# Baseball

# Lacrosse

# 1993-1994

### Football
Overall Record: 3-8
ACC: 2-6

### Women's Soccer
Overall Record: 12-6-3
ACC: 2-1-1
ISAA Ranking: 8th

### Men's Soccer
Overall Record: 15-5
ACC: 4-2
ISAA Ranking: 10th
Soccer America
Ranking: 5th

### Field Hockey
Overall Record: 7-14
ACC: 0-3

### Men's Swimming
Overall Record: 2-7
ACC: 0-3

### Women's Swimming
Overall Record: 6-3
ACC: 0-3

### Wrestling
Overall Record: 7-6
ACC: 0-5

### Volleyball
Overall Record: 30-3
ACC: 14-0
Competed in the Sweet 16
NCAA Tournament
ACC Tournament
Champions

# Athletic Highlights

## Men's Basketball
Overall Record: 28-6
ACC: 12-4
Competed in the Final Four
NCAA Tournament

## Women's Basketball
Overall Record: 16-11
ACC: 7-9

## Track & Field
School Records Set:
4x200 Meter Relay - 1:48.20
4x800 Meter Relay - 9:15.54
Distance Medley Relay - 11:50.04
Shot Put - 40-1 1/4
Triple Jump - 36-9

## Women's Tennis
Overall Record: 19-5
ACC: 8-0

## Men's Tennis
Overall Record: 21-6
ACC: 7-0

## Women's Golf
ACC Championship: 3 of 4
NCAA East Regionals: 2 of 19
NCAA Championships: 4 of 18

## Men's Golf
ACC Championship: 4 of 9
NCAA East Regionals
NCAA Championship

## Baseball
Overall Record: 33-20
ACC: 16-8

## Lacrosse
Overall Record: 10-6
ACC: 1-2

AITS

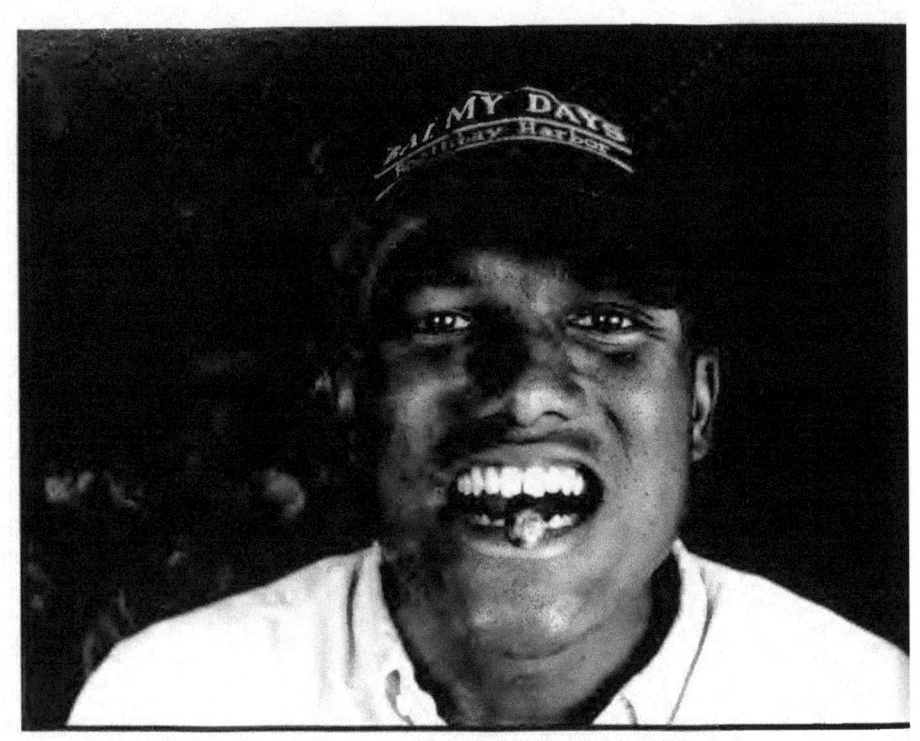

**Kevin Maillard**
President, Class of 1994

**Marisa Dolinsky**
President and Principal Flutist, Duke Wind Symphony

"It is music's lofty mission to shed light on the depths of the human heart."
-Robert Schumann

**Harris Berenson**
Cartoonist

"Fat, drunk, and stupid is no way to go through life, son."
-Vernon Wormer, Dean of Faber College

**Bo King**
Cyclist

**Traci McMillian**
Drum Major, Duke University Marching Band

TO:
cluelessindividual@acpub.duke.edu
CC:
someotherdukie@acpub.duke.edu
FROM: EXXIT@acpub.duke.edu
RE: Monday, Monday this semester was not a guy.

I'm not sure it was using the word 'culottes,' Harris Berenson's delightful drawing of me or the fact that I was never so offensive that I was a feature of letters to the editor that revealed my gender over the semester. But I do know that, despite my efforts to conceal it, the fact that a woman was writing Monday, Monday was no secret to the thousands of clever geniuses who infest this campus.

Although I had some difficulty writing with such double anonymity, I knew I had achieved some success when I started to overhear myself being referred to as both he and she. Which, actually, was fine with me, as long as people weren't insinuating that I know all there is to know about the crying game.

A note to Monday, Monday wannabes for next semester: When filling out the application about how you will differ from past Monday, Mondays, anyone who referred to EXXIT as "Pat" can start listening to Lubricated Goat, because I will see to it that compiling the WXDU Top Ten List for R&R will be the only writing you'll be doing for The Chronicle next year.

Some people have asked me whether being the first female Monday, Monday has meant anything special to me. Over cappucino at The Cafe recently, Nan and I discussed what it meant to be pioneering women of Duke. As I told Nan, being a woman has brought me special advantages to writing this column. I know what it's like to have had the opportunity to just say no to clogs and I know what it's like to have been the one wearing the sorority rush nametag, not just the one making fun of it.

Best of all, so far as I know, I've been the only Monday, Monday to have had the privilege of using the women's bathroom in Cameron. (Guys, if you've never seen them, check them out, brass fixtures, marble countertops--makes the Washington Duke look like the Rockin' K). Somehow, I don't think Nan was impressed by my insight. I was pleased, though, because the most intellectual conversation I had engaged in previously with Nan was at the senior class BBQ; it consisted entirely of, "Oh, what funny looking hushpuppies, don't you think?"

Why "EXXIT"? I know many of you titans of science have already figured this one out by now, but for those of you who have never set foot on Science Drive and--I shudder at the thought--have never been awed by the way Dr. Bonk can light up the actinide series, the two Xs refer to the two X chromosomes all mammalian female cells contain. If you are a pre-med who took the MCAT on Saturday and failed to pick up on this all semester, I know who you are and I have already notified AMCAS to deduct a point from your biological sciences section.

I received suggestions from multiple sources for a nom de plume, based on variations on my name, my initials or nicknames. But somehow, VULCAN MIND PROBE (bad memories of a 21st birthday at Sat's), RADIOLABELLED DNA PROBE (too bio-nerdy), WHAT A JAP! (I don't own a 325i convertible) and especially FAMILY JULES (no comment on the wiseass who thought of that one) just weren't the pennames I was looking for.

I chose the word "exit" because of the state from which I hail, the hom of horrendous highways, hypodermics, high hair and the Hurleys-- New Jersey. For four years, I have had to put up with the worst NJ-bashing jokes, including "You from Jersey, what exit?" (hence the nam and comments from oh-so-funny Pegramites my freshman year that my roommate Dorothy, a fellow Garden State native, and I had created an ozone hole over East Campus with all the hair spray we used.

Okay, at this point in my Duke career, I am willing to admit to anyone with a class of '94 pig boo! that yes, there was a time in my li before I made the realization that when it comes to hairdos, quality more important than quantity. Le this serve as proof to some dear friends who formerly believed tha could dish it out but I couldn't tak it. Not only were they wrong, the were never funny until they met r

Before I finish, I have a few than yous that need mention. To Adel Brooke, Kelly, Liza and Ben, for th ideas, their critiques and their bei, the worst liars, no matter howmu they were harassed by suspicious individuals (Pooh). To Em and Rotty, who were among my origi encouragers. To Ginny and Reill and other friends I never told, wl never thought twice when I said, "No, I never read Monday, Mond this semester. I think he sucks."

Like kegs, SPEs, H. Keith H., the Bubble, BOG intellectualism, the ri rider board, the DAP (no wait, scrat that one), the BP, Arthur's and any thing else at Duke that has made its departure in the past four years, Tri senior Julie Probst now makes her g and glorious exxit.

-from The Chronicle, vol. 89, 1993-94

**Julie Probst**
Monday, Monday

## Howard J. Wesley

Nigger, Negro, Colored, African-American, Black
    How many things can I be at once?
Spook, Coon, Nigger, Monkey, Quota
    How many insults must I carry at once?
"Equal But Separate", Black Faculty Initiative, Rodney King
    How many injustices must I face at once?

The African-American's legacy has always been one of less than or unequal to. I didn't come from a rich, plush background. I was never sheltered from the realities of being Black. Life is hard enough as it is when people think your skin is too dark to be treated fairly. But the problem becomes twice as bad when you're constantly looking for racism and prejudice. The harder you search for racism the more likely you'll find it and eventually you'll become that which you are searching for.

Some people think I'm involved in too many things but everything ain't beautiful in this Gothic Wonderland. The most important thing I'm taking with me, as I leave Duke, is that anything broken, including people's thoughts, can be fixed if you stop staring at the problem and start working towards repair. Anyone who sees a wrong and lets it remain a wrong has become part of the wrong.

                                              Peace Out, Phi Nupe
                                                      Howse

## Susan B. Anthony Somers-Willett
Feminist poet/artist/activist

POET UNDERGOES PLASTIC SURGERY

The doctor showed me all the different noses
he could attach.
I chose the one like an ear.

I suppose my face wanted to listen
but what did my face want to say?

I want to tell him before I go under

You may open my face
and find this:
a smile, a pen, a knife.

**Janet Johnson**
Tenaj, Jeanette, Jan-o

**George**
Roommate

## Ted "klem" Snyderman
### R&R Editor

I find it hard/To believe you don't know/The beauty that you are
But if you don't/Let me be your eyes/A hand to your darkness/So you won't be afraid
I'll be your mirror/ Reflect what you are/ In case you don't know.
--The Velvet Underground

And really how simple it all is: in one day, in one hour, everything could be arranged
at once! The main thing is to love your neighbor as yourself -- that is the main thing,
and that is everything, for nothing else matters.
-- "Dream of a Ridiculous Man," Fyodor Dostoyevsky

It's easy to become a satallite today without even being aware of it. This country can seduce God. Yes it has that seductive power of dollarism. You can cuss out colonialism, imperialism and all other kinds of isms, but it's hard for you to cuss that When they drop those dollars on you, your soul goes.
--Malcolm X

society is a hole it makes me lie to my friends . . .
my friends are girls wrapped in boys - we're living in pieces
i want to live in peace - society is a hole
--Sonic Youth

UNLESS
-- The Lorax

**Antonio Minchella**
Construction Supervisor, Duke Team of Habitat Volunteers

**Alex Hartemink**
Rhodes Scholar

**Keir Morton, Vanessa Davis, Karen Piper, Tiffany Speaks**
Campus Activists and Women's Studies Dorm Residents

**Jane Small**
Pisces Volunteer

**Amy Adler & Agrippa**
<u>Homo</u> <u>sapien</u> & <u>Propithicus</u> <u>tattersalli</u>

**Marjorie Menza**
President of Women's Health Peer Educators

**Mev Maxon & Royal**
President, Duke Equestrian Team

**Nicole Pittman**
Member, Women's Track Team

**Tenten Wu & Lara Shalov**
Co-Presidents, DUMA Student Art Volunteers

**Ted Hull**
Chair, Major Attractions
Duke University Union

RESIDEN

TIAL LIFE

## House A

## Alspaugh

## Arts (Mitchell Tower)

**Aycock**

**Bassett**

**Bedrock**

**Broughton**

**Brown**

**House CC**

**Campus Oaks**

**Canterbury**

**House D**

1111 Urban

Epworth

Fubar

**House G**

**Gilbert Addoms**

**Giles**

**House H**

**Halfway House**

**Hanes**

### Hanes Annex

### Hastings

### H.O.H.

### Jarvis

### Lancaster

### Languages (Decker Tower)

**Maxwell House**

**Mirecourt**

**House P**

Residential Life•187

Pegram

Round Table

Scott House

**611 Watts**

**Southgate**

**Spectrum**

### Stonehenge

### Stratford

### 317 East Trinity

Trent

Wannamaker I

Wannamaker III

## Wannamaker IV

## Wayne Manor

## Windsor

**House YW**

**Central Campus**

**Central Campus**

Residential Life • 195

LIFE

**Alpha Delta Pi**

**Alpha Epsilon Phi**

**Alpha Epsilon Pi**

## Alpha Kappa Alpha

## Alpha Phi

## Alpha Phi Alpha

Alpha Tau Omega

Alpha Omicron Pi

Beta Theta Pi

**Chi Omega**

**Delta Delta Delta**

**Delta Gamma**

Delta Kappa Epsilon

Delta Sigma Phi

Delta Sigma Theta

### Delta Tau Delta

### Kappa Alpha

### Kappa Alpha Theta

### Kappa Kappa Gam

### Kappa Sigma

### Omega Psi Phi

**Phi Delta Theta**

**Phi Kappa Psi**

**Pi Beta Phi**

Pi Kappa Alpha

Pi Kappa Phi

Psi Upsilon

**Sigma Alpha Epsilon**

**Sigma Chi**

**Sigma Nu**

## Sigma Phi Epsilon

## Theta Chi

## Zeta Tau Alpha

1994

Jeffery Aaron
Teos S. Abadia
Stephen C. Abate
Zaid Abdul-Aleem
Betsy V. Ackerson
Allison Adin

Amy P. Adler
Sanders L. Adu
Chris C. Affolter
Margaret E. Ahlin
Vinita Ahuja
Heather C. Ainsworth

Eric M. Albert
Jamil Albertelli
Eric S. Albright
Todd R. Albright
Sunil M. Alexander
Theonie J. Alicandro

Cathleen D. Allen
Helen P. Allen
Marni L. Allen
Frantz E. Alphonse
Dana Y. Al-Shirawi
Cannon C. Alsobrook

Clay W. Amerault
Eric W. Amundson
Scott R. Andersen
Christina H. Anderson
Matthew J. Anderson
Melissa D. Anderson

Nicole R. Anderson
Jinky C. Ang
Mary Ann Annunziata
Sarah K. Appen
Geoffrey Archer
Agustin R. Arellano

Jane K. Armstrong
Michael D. Armstrong
Robert T. Armstrong
Craig S. Arneson
Bridgett M. Arnold
Mark P. Arnold

Deborah L. Arscott
Glen M. Arwk
Susannah L. Arwood
Kibwe J. Ashton
Zarena D. Aslami
Ashley Atkins

Scott N. Atwood
David J. Augustine
Claire E. Aulicino
Elizabeth P. Austen
David P. Ayers
Sara L. Ayres

Mark Baccei
Benjamin M. Bahk
Stephanie R. Bailenson
Clark Bailey
Courtney Bailey
David B. Bailey

Luna D. Bailey
Stephanie A. Bailiff
Frederique C. Bailliard
Karen A. Baim
Alexander M. Bain
Meredith A. Baish

Marshall S. Baker
Melanie A. Baldwin
Robert Baldwin
Natasha B. Ball
Paul E. Bambrick
Kendra L. Bankston

Chris Baptist
Myla D. Barefield
Ashley C. Barfield
Mary N. Barkley
Leslie S. Barna
Rebecca N. Barnhilll

Bethany A. Barratt
Alisa O. Barrett
Mark G. Barrett
Shannon M. Barrett
Ayanna K. Barrow
Rob Barry

John T. Bashore II
Todd T. Bashore
Nicole A. Basile
Joshua C. Batkin
Daniel E. Bauer
Joel S. Bauman

Sheela N. Bavikatty
Sara M. Baylis
Robert H. Beach
Laura R. Beasley
Jonathan D. Becker
Shawn E. Beckerman

Class of 1994•213

David S. Belardo
Bridgit S. Bell
Nicholas P. Bell
Anthony J. Bellezza
Sharla A. Benjamin
Allan Bennett

Blaine A. Benson
Lara S. Benton
Andrew E. Benzing
Brett Berenchak
Harris T. Berenson
Jessica B. Berg

Deborah L. Berger
Elizabeth K. Berghausen
Shari A. Berke
Jodi E. Berlin
Emily A. Berman
Melissa I. Bermudez

Jason M. Bernhardt
Benjamin M. Bernstein
Erin D. Berryman
Lesley A. Berson
Rachel Bertin
Thomas Beshere

Emily H. Betz
John R. Betz Jr.
Joshua C. Bienfang
Alan M. Bienstock
Jennifer M. Biggs
Michael Bingle

Jaye E. Bingham
Laura A. Bishop
Megan J. Bishop
Dara R. Blachman
Robert J. Blackwell
Amy L. Blair

Thomas W. Blake
Jonathan N. Bland
William J. Blanke
Brian D. Blatt
Scott Bles
Heidi D. Blickenstaff

Julia A. Blohm
Kurt M. Bloomhuff
Tonya N. Blosser
Denise A. Blythe
Abigail B. Boardman
Jennifer L. Boisture

Hillary A. Bollam
Joseph M. Bollinger
Franc Boltezar
Michael W. Booze
Travis P. Boozer
Jane E. Borcherding

Tanisha R. Bostick
Kate Bostock
Michael C. Bosworth
Matthew C. Bouchard
Brooke W. Bowman
Ted Boyse

Joseph M. Braceland
Timothy J. Bradford
Daniel R. Brady
Sally M. Brand
Anne H. Bransten
Justin S. Brennan

Sharon L. Brenner
Susan M. Breslin
Kenneth S. Bring
Clifton L. Brinson
Rachel L. Brod
Sage R. Brody

Alisha L. Brosse
Colin C. Brown
Douglas M. Brown
Franchesca D. Brown
Jeannine S. Brown
Brooke E. Browne

Susan E. Bruce
Marshall S. Brunson
Debra Bryant
Matthew M. Buchanan
Kristin E. Bucher
David A. Buchsbaum

Robin S. Buck
Raviender Bukkapatnam
Scott B. Bullock
David G. Bundy
Sonja C. Burban
Cynthia Burks

LaVias M. Burns
Douglas G. Bush
Henry F. Butehorn III
Benjamin T. Butler
C. Hardy Butler
Elizabeth F. Butler

John K. Buuck
Tiffany A. Buxton
Alicia S. Byrd
Robert S. Cady
Timothy R. Cain
Amy L. Cairney

MaryAnne Callan
Angelica M. Calzetta
David A. Cameron
Nedra D. Campbell
Travis Campbell
Stewart M. Campbell

Christopher G. Canonico
Jonathan R. Cantor
John Cardosa II
Martine A. Carlson
Stephen C. Carmac
Mark W. Carmean

James L. Caroland
John E. Carreyrou
Jill H. Cartwright
WilliamB. Carver
Kimberli A. Cary
Lisa C. Case

Amy L. Cassara
Marc Cavan
Erik C. Cehrs
Margaret E. Cervin
Pinar Ceyhan
Peter Cha

Alida R. Chack
Christian H.Chandler
Damon B. Chandler
Benjamin G. Chang
Eunjoo K. Chang
Fay W. Chang

Gary C. Chang
Roger K. Chang
Wayne W. Chang
Vanessa Chartouni
Cherin M. Chaykowsky
Joey Chen

Justin S. Chen
Barry Cheng
Pritha Chitkara
Eric K. Chiu
David W. Choate
Keri L. Christensen

Micky J. Chun
Charles H. Chung
Gary Chung
Kristen E. Chute
Jaime Cintado
Chad M. Clark

Sarah M. Clark
Stephen M. Clarke Jr.
Candace E. Clary
Michael R. Clayton
Brian S. Clise
Louis S. Clyburn

Ashley A. Clymer
Paula L. Coates
Lawrence P. Cogswell III
Greta Y. Cokley
Matthew J. Colangelo
Brian T. Colbert

Karen E. Coleman
Sana D. Coleman
James H. Collins
Paula M. Collins
John P. Conery
Cristin A. Conley

Catherine Conrad-Saydah
Christopher M. Conway
Alyson J. Cook
Kareem A. Cook
Norman L. Cook
Leika M. Cooke

Mark J. Cooper
Scott T. Cooper
Russell B. Copeland
Christopher R. Cormier
Eric C. Correll
Daniel Cortez

R. Eric Cotte
Lydia R. Coulter
Nicole M. Coute
Kayrn R. Couvillion
Christopher L. Cowger
Jennifer K. Cox

Michele E. Cox
Timothy J. Cox
James P. Creighton
Aaron T. Crewse
Stacy L. Crickmer
Matthew W. Crossland

Class of 1994•217

Catherine Crutcher
Emily H. Culver
Lora G. Cummings
Joseph P. Cunningham
Jennifer M. Curley
Daniel A. Curnow

Carolyn A. Cutney
Christopher A. Dales
Richard C. D'Alonzo
Kellie K. Daniels
Lisa E. Daniels
Sean J. Daniels

Pamela A. Daquila
Thomas K. Darlington
Carin B. Daugherty
Julie A. Daumit
Michael A. Dauphinais Jr.
Charles W. Davenport

Taylor M. Davenport
Gregory S. Davidson
Julie J. Davidson
Brendan M. Davies
Caroline S. Davis
Cristina E. Davis

Dana L. Davis
Dilsey M. Davis
Nechole Davis
Patricia L. Davis
Rob Davis
Robert E. Davis

Vanessa L. Davis
Julia A. Dawes
Kenneth D. Dawson
Wendy E.P. Day
Dagny I. de la Peña
Dave A. DeVito

Alice Dealey
James R. Dean
Karen S. Dean
Elizabeth A. DeBartolo
David N. DeBoe
Julie C. DeBolt

Julie A. DeCamp
Edith E. DeKock
Clarissa M. del Mundo
Michael K. Delano
John J. Delves
Cheska Demars

Daniel D. Demeyts
Buckley K. Dempsey
Catherine M. Dent
David J. DePerro
Anne P. Deprince
Keith E. Derman

Louise J. Despard
Cory L. Destribats
Sandesh Dev
Garrett J. DeYulia Jr.
Rahul S. Dhumale
Janet V. Diaz

Kendreia DIckens
Robert W. Dickey
William F. Dietz
Liza A. DiLeo
Raegan Diller
Albert C. DiMeo

Robert T. DiNardo
Bennett W. Dixon
Katrin H. Doane
Margaret Dolan
Shelly R. Dolev
Marisa C. Dolinsky

Carlos A. Dominguez
Jennifer A. Dominguez
Michael J. Donnelly
Rebecca S. Dopp
N. Bernard Dorsey Jr.
Stanley K. Dorsey

Christine H. Dovey
Kirk C. Downey
Stephanie E. Doval
Colleen E. Doyle
Teri L. Drean
Richard S. Dreger

Jeffrey H. Drichta
J. Christopher Dries
Marcus D'Silva
Christopher R. Duggar
Edward A. Dunn
Jennings F. Durand

Stefan A. Dyckerhoff
Robert C. Eastridge
Scott C. Eckel
Caroline M. Edelen
Dwayne Edwards
Jason L. Ekedahl

Class of 1994•219

Jennifer K. Elder
Scott A. Elder
Katherine L. Elliott
Dorothy G. Ellis
Brian M. Embon
Chris S. Endy

Edlyn Q. Engle
Thomas A. Enstice
Heather E. Epes
Lori B. Epps
Geoffrey R. Erickson
Craig L. Eskay

Thomas K. Espy
Kimberly A. Estler
Marci R. Etter
John S. Ettinger
Corey D. Evans
Frederick G. Evans

Marne K. Evans
Valerie J. Evans
Jennifer K. Ewing
Jill C. Ewing
Robyn R. Fader
Melissa C. Fair

Olayinka V. Fajana
Wei-Han H. Fang
Angela L. Fannon
Gregory S. Farley
John C.M. Farquhar
Dana Farver

Kenneth C. Fasanaro
Thomas E. Favazza
Kimberly D. Faw
Virginia M. Fay
Sandi G. Feaster
Dennis Feenaghty

Michael J. Feiler
Matthew T. Feldman
Tracy J. Feldman
Christen E. Feldmann
Billy D. Felton
David A. Feruson

Kevin M. Ferguson
Miguel E. Fernandez
Sergio R. Ferreira
Lisa G. Ferri
Jessica G. Few
Joseph Finarelli

Alexander D. Fine
J. Erick Fink
David J. Finley
Kathleen E. Finnegan
Nicholas A. Fiore
Jonathan H. Fish

Julie A. Fishman
Jill R. Fishow
James M. Fitts
Christopher F. Flaherty
George I. Flatau
Joel L. Fleck

Jennifer L. Fleisher
Alicia S. Fletcher
Rebecca L. Fletcher
Kymberly N. Floyd
Patricia A. Flynn
Mark J. Follman

Tanya L. Forsheit
Sharon C. Forth
John M. Fortune
Erik W. Foss
Alexander Fox
Eric H. Fox

Jennifer L. Fox
Steven H. Frank
J. Robert Frederick
Diane E. Freeman
Julie D. Freeman
Chrissy Frey

Max J. Friedauer
Gregory R. Friedman
Jason S. Friedman
Brian N. Frisch
Alicia S. Fuchs
Monique L. Fuguet

Robert M. Fulghum
Mark A. Funaki
Nadia A. Gaafar
Nicholas E.O. Gaglio
Kyle C. Gaines
Theodore E. Galanthay

Jeffrey C. Galaska
Joan M. Gallagher
Maria Garci
Cindy R. Gardner
Kristine L. Garrett
Cecelia A. Gassner

Class of 1994•221

Josh K. Gelerter
Steven K. Geller
Laura C. Gentile
Clare N. Gentry
Cynamon K. Gentzler
Michael D. George

Patrick S. Geraghty
Erik F. Gerding
John D. Germanotta
Louise A. Gerstenfeld
Shawn L. Gerth
Chetan G.O. Ghai

Robert D. Gilbreath
Keith A. Gill
Kristine N. Gilligan
Jodi B. Ginsberg
Michael D. Ginsberg
Thomas P. Gissendanner

Rhonda S. Gittens
Melvyn E. Glusman
Daniel F. Gotfredo
Sanjay Gohil
Joshua L. Goldberg
Nancy B. Goldberg

Mark A. Golden
Dana M. Goldsmith
Jason Goldstein
Jeremy Goldstein
Jesse Goldstein
Rebecca E. Goldstein

Clay W. Goldwein
Dionne R. Gonder
Paul V. Gonzaga
Elizabeth R. Good
Julie R. Goodman
Michael W. Goodman

Paris N. Goodyear
Tayrn S. Gordon
Angela C.S. Gore
Jonathan H. Grabowski
Charles B. Grace
Nicholas E. Grace

Scott Graham
Patrick D. Grant
Deborah C. Graves
Gavin M. Gray
Giovanni G. Graziano
Nicholas I. Graziano III

Mark E. Grazman
Dara A. Green
Lauren L. Green
Shari B. Green
Tamara M. Green
Steven H. Greene

Jennifer R. Greeson
Christine M. Gregorski
Keith W. Grigg
Jeffrey J. Grills
Keasha D. Grindley
Sharon L. Grove

James A. Grover
Nkenge M. Gude
Kelly R. Gunderson
Sean T. Gunning
Suvarna Gupta
Robert J. Haas

Halim M. Habiby
Jonathan L. Hackman
William H. Hadnott
Matt Hafer
Matthew N. Haies
Nicholas N. Haines

Jereemy D. Hajdu
Ziyad S. Hakura
Doug M. Hall
Eric K. Hall
Freeman S. Hall
Christopher S. Hameefman

Earl F. Hamm Jr.
Gayle Han
Alex G. Hanafi
Brooke A. Hanaway
Jennifer Handal
Gregory P. Hanes

Dennis Hanzlik
Kam I. Haq
Joshua L. Hardison
Richard L. Hardon
David H. Hardtke
Brian D. Harkavy

Matthew J. Harkins
Julie E. Harkness
Gray H. Harley
John T. Harmeling
Abigail W. Harmon
Molly B. Harmon

Class of 1994•223

Anne Maria Harocopos
Brian J. Harris
Kenneth R. Harris
Michael P. Harris
Tonya D. Harris
Carrie M. Hart

Deanna Hart
Alexander J. Hartemink
Keith H. Hasson
Jesse P. Haven
Keith J. Hawkins
Gene L. Hayes

Hooly L. Hayes
Robert J. Hayes
Mack N. Haynes
James M. Heckman
Jason N. Hefter
Justin B. Heineman

Brian L. Helm
Ray W. Helms
John J. Helton
Felecia A. Henderson
Donna M. Hendricks
Jeffrey A. Hendrickson

Duane R. Hennion
Brett T. Henrickson
Clarence T. Henry
Erica M. Henry
Lisa M. Hepburn
Braden P. Herman

Sarah E. Herrick
Jared A. Hershberg
Catherine J. Hertzig
Stephen P. Hiel
Kimberly S. Higgins
Christopher G. Hill

C. Mark Hill
Michael D. Hill
Kevin M. Hilton
Adriane C. Hirsch
Justin Hoagland
Shannon M. Hodge

Steve J. Hodges
Charles F. Hogan
Wyatt L. Hogan
Donna Hoghooghi
Joy I. Hogley
William B. Holden

John D. Holly IV
Claire M. Holroyd
Aleicia C. Holt
Travis C. Honeycutt
Amy E. Hood
Jennifer A. Hooker

Elizabeth A. Hooton
Kevin L. Hopper
Kathleen L. Horan
David J. Horowitz
Teague Horton
Alison L. Hosmer

Steven C. House
David B. Howard
Joseph J. Howell
Myriam R. Huber
Deirdre M. Hudson
Kendra A. Hudson

Paul B. Hudson
Geoff L. Hughes
Daniel T. Hull
Susan E. Hulvey
Richard D. Hunter
Angello L. Huong

Lainie J. Hurst
Christopher T. Hurtgen
Edward I. Hwang
Kenneth Imerman
Aissa E. Inskeep
Chris Inzerillo

James M. Iorio
Katherine L. Ivey
Julie S. Ivker
Robert L. Jacks
Dasha Jackson
Russell K. Jackson

Kelly V. Jacob
Lawrence D. Jacobs
M. Joy Jacobs
Neal S. Jacobs
Gautam Jagannathan
Ian M. James

Warren H. James
Kevin E. Jameson
Ralph E. Jankowich
Brian A. Jacquette
Eric C. Jarvis
Gretchen A. Jehle

Class of 1994•225

 M. Jenkins
 D. Jennings
Nancy L. Jennings
Geoff Jenson
Sa mine Jernigan
Tyler P. Jernstedt

Catherine J. Jhee
Adriana M.C. Johnson
Chad R. Johnson
Erik C. Johnson
Janet Johnson
Jawana M. Johnson

Nicole E. Johnson
Rebecca E. Johnson
Robert E. Johnson
Scott D. Johnson
Ellis M. Johnston
Jonathan E. Jones

Laura E. Jones
Laura R. Jones
Peter Jones
David E. Joneschild
Molly K. Joondeph
Elizabeth B. Juda

Raymond A. Jurgens
Katherine P. Kadison
Jeffery H. Kahn
Jeffery Kaiser
Brett D. Kalmowitz
Mizuho Kameoka

Christopher S. Kammer
David Kaplan
Irene Kaplan
David C. Katz
Evan M. Katz
Rebecca D. Katz

Julie E. Keaton
Ayana N. Kee
Paul P. Kelleher
John L. Kelley
Robert J. Kelley
Emily H. Kelly

Julie H. Kern
Sotirous T. Keros
Erin K. Kesterson
Michael G. Khoury
William Kiang
Todd R. Kile

Claire D. Kim
Judy Kim
Simon S. Kim
Sohee M. Kim
Thomas S. Kim
Young Kim

Christina H. King
Gerald W. King Jr.
James W. King
Jason S. King
Vicki C. King
Christopher G. Kirby

Carrie S. Kithianis
Aaron Kitlowski
Sunny A. Klaber
Neil C. Klaproth
Adam N. Klein
Daniel W. Koenig

Jeffery A. Komisarof
David S. Konczal
James A. Kong
E-Bai Koo
John R. Koon
Tonia M. Korves

Karen L. Kossack
Brian F. Kowal
Andrew Konop
Thomas J. Krackeler
David J. Krauss
Seth R. Krawitz

Margaret E. Krendl
Miriam S. Kriegel
Christy Kroeger
Stephanie L. Krolick
Nancy Krolikowski
Carolyn L. Kroovand

Milele L. Kudumu
Eddie Kulkamthorn
John C. Kuo
Andrew A. Lago
Elizabeth P. LaGuardia
Roma Lal

Megan E. Lamb
Judy K. Land
David A. Landsman
Nancy M. Langdon
Christopher D. Lansford
Ronald A.A. Lapid

Class of 1994•227

Eric J. Lapidus
Kristen S. Larsen
Jeffrey S. Laufenberg
Julia M. Laurenzano
Kara L. Lavender
Stephanie J. Lawkins

Jennifer Le Blanc
Jeffrey M. Leavitt
Abraham K.H. Lee
Albert Lee
Arnold Lee
Christine D. Lee

Christopher A. Lee
Frank Lee
Janice Lee
Kasey K. Lee
Kenneth Lee
Sandra Lee

Katrina L. Lehtola
Dahna A. Leiser
Tracy C. Lemmon
Scott W. LennonThomas J. Leverton
Joseph A. Levitin

Fleur D. Levitz
David S. Levy
Stuart A. Levy
Janet E. Lewis
Jason A. Lewis
Mary C. Lewis

Rebecca J. Lewis
Joseph L. Lichtenberger Jr
Douglas G. Lichtman
Steven M. Lichtman
Jennifer K. Licker
Sarah A. Lieberman

Melvin V. Limson
Dean D. Lin
John L. Lin
Richard K. Lin
Holly K. Link
Eva D. Littman

Owen S. Littman
Ann B. Lockhart
Henry A. Long II
Jeremy A. Long
Michaela L. Long
Alice H. Loo

228

Patrick D. Lopath
Elizabeth J. Lorscheider
Brian F. Loss
Abbie L. Lotke
David C. Lott
David M. Love

Michael J. Lovelace
Robert C. Ludeman
Lorraine E. Ludemann
Todd M. Lukasik
Meredith D. Lukoff
John M. Luongo

Jeffery S. Lutz
Justin D. MacFarlan
Kristin M. Mack
Richard B. Madden
Suhas Madhiraju
Shannon J. Magglo

Juliana L. MaGill
Stephanie L. Maher
Bo M. Mahoney
Brian S. Mahoney
Kevin M. Maillard
Colin C. Mailloux

David R. Malin
Robin L. Maloof
William J. Mandel
Jennifer D. Manning
Lisa C. Mansell
Julie A. Marcus

Eve E. Marhafer
Jennifer M. Marik
Wayne T. Markowitz
David L. Marks
D. Brent Marshall
Sarah E. Martin

Joe M. Martinez
Claudio Martonffy
Valerie L. Marx
William J. Maschke
James M. Mason
Shannon M. Mason

Kathleen J. Master
Mauro M. Mastrapasqua
Michael J. Mathers
Krista Mathisen
Karen E. Matsushima
Thomas B. Matthews

Class of 1994•229

Roger M. Massingham
Marianne Maw
Mev Maxon
Christopher L. May
Nancy D. Mazor
Andrew M. McAlpin

Jennifer S. McCall
Jason L. McCandless
William M. McClatchey Jr.
Matthew W. McCleskey
Carol McConnel
Kathleen M. McCue

Leonard N. McCullough
Jane P. McFadden
Jeanne B. McFeely
Michael A. McGarry
Randall E. McGeorge
Scott E. McIntosh

Hillary R. McKinney
Kevin C. McMains
Pamela D. McMains
Tracy D. McMillian
Kelsey E. McNabb
Sean McNally

Michael S. McNamara
Valerie Y. McNeil
Kevin M. McNulty
Kara L. McShane
Kelly A. Mead
Joseph A. Mecia

Miles E. Medrano
Dallas E. Meeker
Katherine L. Melcher
Sarah Mervine
Cade P. Metz
Heather H. Meyer

Michael R. Meyer
Dina E. Meyers
Deborah M. Michael
Emily J. Michael
Daniel H. Michaels
Stephanie B. Michaud

Suzanne C. Michelson
Michelle L. Middleton
Joseph M. Milano
Robert M. Milazzo
Thomas M. Miles
Brian C. Miller

Emily L. Miller
Scott C. Miller
Emily E. Milliken
Antonio Minchella
Megan E. Mingey
Romana Moezzi

Stephen L. Mott
Nimish A. Mohile
Jennifer R. Mohr
Julia K. Molise
Mark K. Moller
Marcello M. Mollo

Aimée N. Molloy
Jon Molner
William J. Monroe
Mark J. Montano
Maria P. Montenora
Amanda K. Montgomery

Liam J. Montgomery
Lee Katherine Moore
Maisie S. Moore
Susan B. Moore
Katheryn Moreira
Elizabeth C. Morgan

Sharon D. Morgan
Julie A.S. Morison
Richard Morris
Jason B. Mortimer
Keir D. Morton
David I. Mosse

Fionna Mowat
Dean F. Moyar
Michael P. Muehr
Evan M. Mueller
Lauren S. Mullaney
Kevin E. Mullen

Stephen Murphy
John P. Murnane
Thomas P. Murphy
Brian W. Murray
Karna Murthy
Vikram V. Murthy

Chris Myers
Latha Naganna
Radhika D. Naidu
Frances E. Naisang
J. Nicholas Napoli
Masashi Narita

[illegible] Nash
[illegible] L. Neaton
Matthew J. Neidell
Christine B. Nelson
Howard G. Nelson
Plymouth D. Nelson

Rebecca L. Nelson
Sherry V. Nelson
Dmitry Nemirovsky
Katherine J. Nesbitt
Christine L. Neuman
Robert T. Neuner

Nancy H. Newman
Kimberley A. Nicholls
Brian J. Nichols
James L. Nichols
Shawntay T. Nickelson
Tom W. Niemiller

Tamara J. Nix
Carolyn E. Nobel
Zachary Noffsinger
Ryan T. Northrup
Heather L. Norton
Tara L. Norton

Jana M. Novak
Tate Nurkin
Holly K. Ober
Karen O'Connell
Kari A. O'Connell
Ryan O'Connell

James P. Ottutt Jr.
Julie C. Oh
Matthew S. Oliva
Jennifer A. O'Neal
Alexandra P. Orban
Timothy P. O'Reilly Jr.

Federick F. Origenes
Nancy C. Orr
Paul J. Orsulak
Carolyn S. Osmun
Leslie A. Otto
Erik C. Owens

Susan A. Pace
Richard Pacetti
Dongkwan J. Pak
Adam J. Palmer
Matthew L. Pangaro
Brandee L. Pappalardo

232

Demetra D. Pappas
Carol C. Park
Jason J. Park
Matthew T. Parker
Amanda K. Parks
Lisa R. Parrish

Jonathan P. Parsons
Joseph M. Pastore
Aparna N. Patel
Neepa S. Patel
Jarrod M. Patten
Stephen R. Pattillo

Allison A. Paulen
Alison C. Pauly
Peter V.A. Pavlacka
Shannon M. Pazur
Mark A. Peeler
Heidi Pellerano

Richard L. Pensinger
James M. Peppe
Shea M. Pepper
Annalisa B. Perez
Elizabeth Perez
Jack B. Perkins

Michael T. Perlberg
Jennifer L. Perry
Amanda Persaud
Catherine M. Peshkin
Melanie M. Pettway
Malcolm W. Peverley Jr

Simon P. Pharr
Susan S. Philip
M. Vanessa Phillips
Chad E. Piacenti
Jeffrey E. Pierce
Amy Pigott

John Pina III
Laura B. Pinsky
Karen R. Piper
Kenneth J. Pippin
Joanna M. Pitt
Nicole I. Pittman

Robert J. Platt
Audra M. Plenys
Michelle L. Poblete
Melanie S. Pogach
Cecile J. Politte
Juanita L. Pollard

Class of 1994•233

James B. Poole
Lukus J. Porkert
William E. Porter
Adam J. Posner
Jennifer E. Pottheiser
Stephen J. Pratt

Michael W. Prentiss
Todd S. Presner
Michael T. Prewett
Lois Price
Shari L. Principio
Tiffani J. Pringle

Julie A. Probst
Heather E. Prochnow
Chris M. Prosise
Anne Marie E. Puckhaber
Nancy C. Pugh
Gabriel E. Pulido

Gloria Radeff
Erica J. Radlott
Christopher C. Ragona
Shane P. Raley
Heath C. Ramsey
Robert C. Randolph

Alan Rankin
James J. Rapp
Lauren G. Rasmus
Pamela S. Ratliff
Warren L. Ratliff
Jill C. Rau

Katherine A. Ray
Stuart W. Rayburn
Kristi J. Ravimond
Bryan T. Raynor
Charles P. Read
Michael L. Reams

Helen M. Redwine
Amy E. Reed
John C. Reed
LaDonya M. Reed
Declan A. Reid
Nicloe A. Reid

Jamie L. Reitfel
Jennifer L. Reilly
Patrick S. Reinfried
Antoinette M. Reinhart
Leif W. Reinstein
Charles Renz

Erika J. Reutzel
Melissa Reyes
Timothy R. Rich
Todd Rich
Katherine J. Richardson
Maureen E. Richardson

Kyle Y. Ridaught Jr.
Stefanie A. Rider
Alana Ridge
Justin A. Ries
Jeffrey P. Rieth
Stacey J. Rind

Amanda K. Riseden
Allison L. Roads
George E. Robbins
Claudia W. Roberson
David A. Roberts
Monica Roberts

Scott B. Roberts
Kimberly A. Robertson
Katina N. Robinson
W. Walker Robinson
William P. Robinson
Elizabeth H. Rocovich

Andrea R. Roddy
Jennifer A. Rohde
Jennifer L. Rohr
Jennifer L. Rohrig
Theodore D. Rolf
Tanya L. Rolle

Timothy J. Roller
Christopher B. Romig
Dana Romita
David L. Ronquillo
Sean W. Rooney
James A. Rosemond

Wendy Rosenberg
Dawn T. Rosenblum
Laura Rosenstein
Matthew A. Rosenstein
Mohammad R. Rostami
Jason A. Rotman

Michael D. Rouch
David Royster
Brad W. Rubin
Kara A. Rubin
Jonathan E. Rucker
Andrew W. Rudge

Class of 1994 • 235

[illegible] Rudisill
Daniel A. Ruotolo
Haila K. Rusch
John M. Russo
Nancy R. Ryan
Christopher W. Rydberg

Bethany Sacks
Rachel L. Sagan
Jo-Ellen R. Sakowitz
Josh A. Saland
Alphonso J. Salley
Christopher R. Salter

Danielle A. Salus
John M. Sampson
Robert G. Santos
Amy Saperstein
Charles D. Sapp
Shiva Sarraf-Yazdi

Jennifer M. Sarrica
Meredith R. Sasser
Susan E. Sasser
Michael H. Saul
Suzanne E. Saunders
Craig S. Savage

Justin T. Sawyer
Jason G. Sayat
Jonathan G. Sayat
David J. Scanlan
Ryan T. Scarborough
Richard J. Schaen

Rebecca J. Schaffer
James D. Schall
Robert C. Scherer
Dawn A. Scheve
Laura J. Schick
Robert V. Schiess

Marjorie A. Schiff
Carrie E. Schliemann
Mary S. Schneeberger
Jonathan A. Schneider
Carlyle R. Schomberg
Tara N. Schooley

Glen M. Schumacher
Katie H. Schwarting
Jeanette M. Schwartz
Suzanne M. Schwartz
Katie M. Schweiger
Ron R. Sciandri

Jared A. Sclove
Inara K. Scott
LeAnn Scott
Brian T. Scully
Thomas B. Sellers Jr.
Anne R. Sempowski

Matthew G.J. Senfield
Dev K. Sethi
Neil K. Sethi
Noppon P. Setji
Amit E. Shalev
Lara M. Shalov

Meghan G. Shanaphy
Virginia A. Shank
Vijay Shanker
Andrew I. Shapiro
Margaret F. Sharp
Pamela M. Sharpe

Michael A. Shaw
Yvette E. Shenouda
Stephanie A. Sheps
Anne C. Sherman
Bradley J. Sherrod
Roshni Shetty

Amy H. Shields
Joseph B. Shiffler
George Shih
Daniel W. Shima
Jennifer L. Shoda
Melanie Shoffner

Matthew Sidman
Aaron J. Siebeneck
Jonathan B. Siegwl
Neil S. Siegel
Heather L. Signon
Rachel A. Silberberg

Jeremy C. Silverman
Jonathan R. Silverman
Michelle R. Silverstein
Jonathan J. Simon
Marie-Joelle Simonpietri
Adrian H. Simpson

Mark C. Sims
Jeffrey S. Sinclair
Robin Sindler
Stephen B. Sitrin
Jason M. Skaggs
Chad Skinner

Margaret ? Slagel
Mark ? Slominski
Jaime A. Smarr
Adelle M. Smith
April A. Sith
Erica A. Smith

Gary N. Smith
Geoffrey S. Smith
Jennifer C. Smith
Jill S. Smith
Marcus J. Smith
Margaret E. Smith

Najwa D. Smith
Sigma Smith
Stephen C. Smith
Charles K. Smoak
Jamie L. Snow
Brad M. Snyder

Ted B. Snyderman
Terence M. Sobolewski
John Socha
James R. Sokolowski
Christina M. Solters
Michelle D. Somers

Steven F. Somers
James A. Sonne
Jennifer D. Sonnenberg
Carsten M. Sorensen
Carolyn A. Souryal
Claire L. Southern

Timothy J. Sovich
Joy M. Spangler
Vanessa S. Spann
Tiffany M. Speaks
Alan M. Speert
Kara M. Spencer

Jocelyn S. Sperling
Kate A. Sphar
Karen M. Spock
Claude Springfield
Steve O. Spurrier
Mark D. Squillante

Serene S. Srouji
Heather M. Stack
Nathan L. Stacy
Martin Stalheim
Robin J. Stanley Jr.
Stephanie L. Stansbury

238

Wendy J. Stanton
Gregory E. Staton
Renee A. Stavros
Jeffrey B. Steadman
Marnie C. Steele
Meghan E. Steele

Valerie A. Steer
Neil A. Steiner
Michael A. Steinig
Heidi Steltzer
Heather M. Stephens
Joanna T. Stern

David M. Stetson
Andrew R. Stewart
Kristin L. Stewart
Stephanie Stitzer
Joshua M. Stolker
Travis L. Stork

Robert G. Storrs
Thomas L. Story
Carter R. Stowell
James T. Stowell
Chris Streck
Carole L. Strickland

Michael R. Stroeh
Rebecca F. Stults
Chad C. Sturgill
Aaron K. Styer
Kevin K. Sullivan
John W. Sumner

Mary H. Sumner
Varuth I. Suwankosai
Heather M. Swain
Elizabeth S. Swanson
Kathlene C. Swanson
David W. Swayne

Matthew D. Swecker
Ellen F. Swennes
Ernest Sykes
Shawn P. Syron
Ursula M. Szmulowicz
Tricia S. Tang

Michelle L. Tanner
Cheryl L. Tapager
Steven M. Taper
Jenny R. Tart
Marc P. Taurisano
Eugene M. Tay

[names column:]

[illegible] Taylor
[illegible] Michael Taylor
Scott W. Temple
Christopher J. Thacker
Kristie J. Thayer
Adam C. Theiler

Jacqueline D. Thomas
Benetta Y. Thompson
Eric E. Thompson
Kismet Thompson
Lynne N. Thompson
Eddie K. Thorn

Courtney D. Thornburg
Christopher J. Thornton
Sean L. Tibbs
Jennifer L. Tiedeman
James M. Tierney
Daren J. Timmons

Timothy J. Titcomb
Mark Titus
David A. Torgerson
Stacy L. Torian
Nancy E. Torre
Maria A. Towne

Ky Tran-Trong
Eric N. Treschuk
Michael B. Troutman
Blakely K. Tuck
Nathaniel S. Turner
Francisco E. Ullda

Tracy L. Unice
Sarah L. Vaill
Jonathan J. Valen
Anthony D. Valladares
Sarah L. Van Buskirk
Nicole Van Nood

Harriet A. Vance
Jeffrey M. Vanderkam
Talatha Vaughters
Victoria A. Vazquez
Sira Veciana
Andrew T. Vedder

Anita G. Venters
Christopher J. Ventry
Amy Vernick
Jennifer D. Vernon
James P. Vidas
Nick S. Vogenthaler

240

Kevin B. Vosen
Julia D. Vrany
David T. Wafle Jr.
Dustin M. Waide
Hikaru Wajima
Jennifer Waldman

Mary N. Walker
Scott A. Walker
Stacey L. Walker
Brigette D. Wallace
Hope C. Wallace
Robert Waller

Edwin C. Walton III
Christina H. Wang
Henry B. Wang
Jennifer L. Wang
John H. Wang
Victor C. Wang

Samuel L. Ware
Kindra L. Warnecke
George E. Watson
Amy E. Webbink
Leslie L. Weber
Daniel J. Webre

Blair E. Weigle
John H. Weimer
Oscar M. Weiner
Brian S. Weinstein
JoAnne Weiskopf
Jeffrey G. Weiss

Craig C. Welter
Gerald M. Wenner
Stephen H. Wertheim
Howard J. Wesley
Jennifer M. Wesley
Timothy T. West

Katherine I. Whayne
Brian D. Wheeler
Mark D. Whitaker
Chad B. White
Jeffrey L. White
John David R. White

Jennifer D. Whitehead
Tracy R. Whitener
Bridget C. Wiater
Melissa Wiener
Douglas M. Wiese
Arlon Wilber

Ericka N. Wilcher
Timothy W. Wilcox
Keevie Wilder
Michelle L. Wilkins
Bryan T. Williams
Frances H. Williams

Jonathan M. Williams
Thomas M. Williams
Anna F. Wilson
Christopher D. Wilson
Christopher S. Wilson
John M. Wilson

Karen L. Wilson
Kimberly D. Wilson
Kristen A. Wilson
Russell C. Wilson
Steven D. Winch
Jeffrey T. Wingfield

Danielle D. Winkler
Rachel L. Winokur
Jennifer L. Winston
Kerri R. Winter
Alan M. Wise
Matthew W. Wise

John A. Woffington IV
Ira L. Wolfson
Scott G. Womack
Jonathan P. Womer
Sandra S. Won
David Wong

Shannon R. Wong
Hadley M. Wood
Jennifer L. Wood
Lori Wood
Vanessa L. Wood
Rochelle L. Woodbury

Kenneth P. Woodcock
Kristi E. Woods
Astrid Woodward
James R. Wray
Amy L. Wright
Tremaine S. Wright

Tenten Wu
Masahiro A. Yamazaki
Michael N. Yavelberg
Malcolm Yeung
Yin Yin
Maya E. Ynostroza

Lina I. Yoo
Daniel M. Young
Gretchen C. Young
John W. Young
Linda Q. Young
John F. Younger

David K. Yu
Mohamed K. Zanaty
David J. Zavelson
William L. Zee
Alexandra L. Zeland
Marc I. Zemel

Kevin W. Zinck
Heather A. Zuber
David J. Zylstra

In Memoriam
Brian Glenn Wright

One of the most treasured experiences for a faculty member and administrator is the opportunity to know and learn from an ever renewing generation of students. As a Dean, I meet each student at least twice, initially at first year orientation and later at senior year graduation. Some students I have the opportunity to know better than others, of course, and they are the ones from whom I have learned the most and take inspiration. The forums of our interaction range from student government, activities, calling our alumni and friends as part of our Annual Fund drive, projects such as the SAE car designs, career advice to a student applying for graduate school or seeking that important first job, advice from a student to me on how to make our program even better, and in other ways too many to enumerate.

Of all these interactions, the impact of some inevitably stays with me longer and has changed my life in significant ways that I am still sorting out. Last fall, we lost one of our seniors, Brian Wright. I had met Brian as a first year student with the class of 1994. He was a fine scholar from a small town in eastern North Carolina, the pride of his home town and parents. His own father died when Brian was young and his step-father and mother raised him with love and affection. As someone who also lost his father when I was young and who came from a small town in Illinois and went to the national university nearby, I think I may understand some of the joy (and occasional uncertainty) Brian must have experienced when he arrived at Duke. It would have been a special privilege for me to congratulate Brian at our diploma ceremony in the Chapel this spring.

But it was not to be. Brian was lost in a tragic swimming accident. His friends, classmates, parents and family were shocked. How does one explain or understand such an event? Even so, Brian remains a part of my life and yours. He changed Duke as Duke changed him in not altogether knowable ways. And this spring in the Chapel, I and many others will remember, and for many springs to come.

For those of us who have been privileged to form a bond with the class of 1994, no future is possible without remembering.

—Earl Dowell,
Dean of the School of Engineering

Class of 1994•253

# A Senior Story

There's always a story behind the story, so here's mine: until my senior year in high school, I had never heard of Duke University. While the names Oxford, Amherst, Princeton and Harvard danced in my adolescent imagination, the school that would eventually become my alma mater never figured in the over-achieving design of my youth. A few months before applications were due, a copy of the *U.S. News and World Report* college issue fell into my hands (you know the one), and before I knew it, I was in North Carolina.

Arriving as a freshman, I expected nothing. Everything I knew about Duke was hearsay—"hot" college, "hot" English department, "hot" basketball team. Dare I admit this? In many ways, it felt like the university appeared on the face of the planet in order for me to attend. I remember telling a friend on my freshman hall that until the age of six I was convinced that the world was actually an elaborate movie script written for my amusement. "What do you mean until the age of six?" was her response, as I recall. Understandably, she never has let me live this down. But the circumstances of my coming to Duke secretly proved that my six-year-old inner child was right again. *Just like always*, I thought, *you're making it up as you go along*.

Playing master of the universe in my imagination, I honestly believed that these four years might never e[nd]. After nearly two decades of being a student, I've gotten good at it. Yet writing now, less that a month after walking through the successive anticlimaxes of graduation, I jog around East Campus and am surprised by how utte[rly] out of place I feel. Bumping into younger friends in Perkins or the Bryan Center, am I mistaken, or do they all wear the face of someone greeting the terminally ill. *So you're still around? How much longer?*

My sublet is a block from East Campus. I have a summer job that brings me to West Campus five days a

k. Almost every night, I see college friends and the routine still includes Satisfaction's, the Green Room, the ls, Power Company, and Chapel Hill. We still gossip about professors and talk about the future as a hypoth-. Yet a distance quietly settled in that can't be measured with geography; after four years, how strange to be outside, looking in.

I'm beginning to agree with my friend's suspicion that my six-year-old ego maniac never completely grew He's still watching himself star in the role of a lifetime. And writing now, I realize how sorry he is to see the few scenes end. *Leaves home, makes new friends, misses home, has fun, gets smarter, camps out for games, writes mn, falls in love, comes out in column, has more fun, discovers how much more he has to learn. . . .*

I meant to write this essay before I graduated. I wanted to remember Duke like a snapshot, record it ugh words the way this yearbook records it through pictures. But senior year drifted by and I couldn't imag- what I'd say. I worried. My editor worried. And then I began to think about what she always called it, when d nervously ask how my "senior story" was going. When we remember, we tell ourselves, and those who will n, a story. I've often heard it said that when you remember college, you never think of the classes, the tests, the all-nighters. You just remember the people—especially the friends who've made you miserable and made happy, but finally made life better. Memories crowd with people, and you wonder why sometimes these nories turn unexplainably sad. In our memories of Duke, each of us will remember the one person we had to good-bye to at graduation, the person we thought we'd know—and be—forever. We're different people after e, but remembering who we were still makes for a good story.

-Paul Kelleher, Trinity '94, wrote The Chronicle's "Armchair Pundit" column

GUE

homestretch

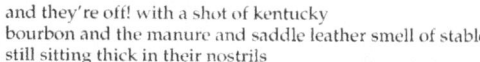

and they're off! with a shot of kentucky
bourbon and the manure and saddle leather smell of stable
still sitting thick in their nostrils

around the first turn damons day takes the lead
the little bald man in the brown pinstripe suit elbows
     his neighbors aside,
wishes he had followed them to visit the grinning man
    in the green booth
(even though everybody knows the lead horse never comes in first)

around the second turn sweat and expectation cloudchoke
tiny yellow tickets curl at the edges, color leaks
    into hands and hands leak color
flowered dresses, legwedded, shoulder past the tulips to send
     red-and-yellow wilting perfumes
    at every windgasp

around the third turn tall glasses of long island iced tea
     and whiskey lemonade sour, watered down and dripping
    with the crowd
under the roarshadow horses' eyes roll back in their heads, whiteblind
    as the jockeys whip them into frenzies
    of win!win!win!

and down the stretch they come!
dreaming, straining, craning for home, they could see it
    if only their eyes wouldn't roll back so far
damons day could see it if he weren't boxed in
    at seventeenth place
the crowd pulls them forward, mindstrings
     stretching to childrens' toys and dog biscuits
     and houses where washed clothes never wave
     across white fences
     where macaroni never spills on the kitchen stove
rolled back eyes for the wife and kids, they say,
    the easydream

the race is over, roanoke wins it
the crowd filters out reluctant - maybe the green board lies
yellow tickets drift in helpless snowfall,
    with lemon rinds, and popcorn bags
coat the sugared grandstand like gatsby's spent party favours

the sweeper rests on his broom, bends down
    and gathers a few to stuff in his pocket
    just in case

                              -Lisa Barnes, Trinity '96

Epilogue • 261

Epilogue • 267

Epilogue • 283

# The Chanticleer Staff

Jen Pottheiser
Athletics Editor

Christina H. Anderson
Editor-in-Chief

Bev Beno
Layout Editor

Derek Thomas
Class of 1994 Editor

Bahar Shapar and Jessica Goldman
Residential and Greek Life Editors

Mike Arlein
Business Manager

Brian Scully
Photographer

Chad Massie, Navin Mahabir, Rich Tarlow, and Alan Chang
Photographers

Nicole Pittman
Photographer

# Photo Credits

**Anderson, Chrissie** - 1, 2a, 3b,c,d,e, 4a,b,c, 10, 12a, 13, 17, 18a, 18c, 20, 21, 22a, 23b, 24a, 24b, 25, 28, 29a, 30, 34, 39, 40b, 41a, 43, 49c, 51b, 52b, 58, 59, 60b, 61a, 64b,c, 66, 67, 71, 72, 73, 75, 76, 77, 78, 79, 81, 86a, 150b, 150d, 152, 159, 162, 164, 168, 170, 171, 174, 175, 176a, 176c, 176d, 181a, 182a, 184b, 185c, 188b, 189a, 190c, 196b,d, 200a, 203a, 204b, 205b, 207a,b, 208b, 209a, 248, 249, 251, 252, 253b, 256b, c, d, 260, 261, 262, 263, 264a, 266, 267, 269, 270a, 273, 274, 277b, 278, 279, 283
**Arlein, Mike**- 60c, 61b, 61c, 86b, 87b
**Allen, Nicole**- 47a
**Barrett, Alisa** - 44a
**Bermudez, Mel** - 3a, 64d, 68, 69, 80, 150a, 153
**Chang, Alan** - 12b, 16a, 178b, 179a,b, 180b, 182b, 183b,c, 186a, 188a, 189b, 198c, 202a, 203b, 281b
**Cades, Deb**- 86c
**Chronicle**- 256a
**Devlin, Joe** - 45a
**Dollar, Luke** - 98, 102b, 125c
**Duke University Photo Department** - 2b, 48, 136, 137
**Gatewood, Hunter**- 86d
**Hendler, Noah** - 44b, 49b,70, 154, 157, 166, 167, 271a, 271c
**Hitchcock, Tigger**- 49a
**Holroyd, Claire**-18b, 22b
**Kao, Ben** - 51a
**Kim, Brian** - 2d
**Laughlin, Jason**- 60a
**Lynn, Doug** - 112, 113, 114, 115
**Mahabir, Navin** - 176b, 178a,c, 179c, 180a,c, 181, 182c, 183a, 184a, 186c, 187, 188c, 189c, 190a,b, 191b,c, 192, 193a, 196a, 199b, 200c, 202b, 206a,c, 208a
**Massie, Chad** - 38, 185b, 186b, 205a, 206b
**Orsulak, Paul** - 46a
**Peterkin, Kirk** - 207c, 253a
**Photo Specialties** - 198a,b, 200b, 201, 203c, 204a, 205c, 208c
**Pincus, David** - 184c, 185a, 191a, 193b,c, 194, 195
**Pittman, Nicole** - 37, 96b, 97a, 101a, 103, 104b, 105a
**Pottheiser, Jen** -19, 26, 27b, 27c, 29b, 36, 45b, 52a, 74, 92, 94, 95, 96a, 97b, 99, 101b, 102a, 105b, 108, 109, 110, 111, 116, 117, 118, 119, 120, 121, 122b, 123, 124, 125a,b, 126, 127, 128, 129, 130, 131, 132, 142, 143, 144, 145, 146, 147, 150c, 155, 156, 160, 163, 172, 173, 196c, 209b,c, 244, 245, 246, 247, 250a, 258, 259, 265, 275, 280, 284
**Poole, Laura** - 42, 47b, 53, 64a, 161, 165, 169
**Rosen, Jamie**- 24c, 271b
**Schall, Jamey** - 40a, 276, 277a, 281a, 282, 288
**Scully, Brian** - 4d, 8, 9, 14, 15, 32, 35, 268, 272
**Serow, Erica**- 87a, 87c
**Shapiro, Andy**- 27a, 264b, 270b
**Tarlowe, Rich** - 100, 104a, 122a, 138, 139, 140, 141
**Taylor, Scott** - 84, 85
**Todd, Les** - 54, 55, 56, 57, 82, 83
**Varden Studios** - 210-243
**Wang, Alex**- 87d
**Woods, Kristie** - 33, 41b, 285

ecial thanks to my family, Tom and Denise Adams, Pauline Myers, Margaret Sartor, Varden Studios, da Studer-Ellis, Lou-Ann Martin-Rogers, Fanny Castillo, and, of course, my friends, who have always en there for me.

duced by Hunter Publishing, Winston-Salem, NC
cover of the 1994 Chanticleer was made with a 150 point Brillantia cover. The end sheets were on 80lb. paper. Senior portraits were taken by Varden dios, Rochester, NY. The black and white photographs in the 10th and 11th signature(s) were duotone PMS Warm Gray 10CV. All black and white photo-ohs were laser-scanned halftones. All color photographs were printed in four color from color transparencies.

opyright 1994, Duke University Undergraduate Publications Board. No parts of this book should be reproduced without express written consent from the rd. All correspondence should be directed to the Chanticleer, 101-3, Bryan Center, Durham, NC 27706 Tel. 919 684 2856.

Lightning Source UK Ltd.
Milton Keynes UK
UKHW011015210820
368606UK00002B/399